JOHN W
QUINTESSE

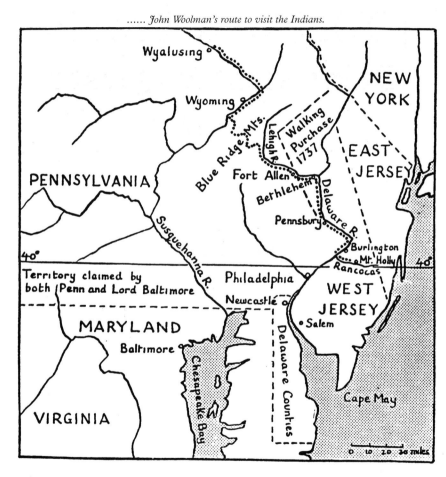

...... John Woolman's route to visit the Indians.

Pennsylvania and New Jersey in the time of Penn and Woolman.
Courtesy Philadelphia Yearly Meeting

JOHN WOOLMAN
Quintessential Quaker
1720 to 1772

by
David Sox

Sessions Book Trust, York, England
in association with
Friends United Press, Richmond, Indiana, USA

© David Sox 1999

UK ISBN 1 85072 218 8

US ISBN 0 944350 43 7

Distributed in North and South America by Friends United Press,
Richmond, Indiana, USA

Library of Congress Cataloging-in-Publication Data
Sox, David.
    John Woolman: Quintessential Quaker, 1720-1772 / by David Sox.
    p.   cm.
    Includes bibliographical references and index.
    ISBN 0-944350-43-7 (US). -- ISBN 1-85072-218-8 (UK)
    1. Woolman, John, 1720-1772. 2. Quakers--United States--
Biography.   I. Title.
BX7795.W7S69   1999
289.6'092--dc21
[B]   99-17820
                                                                       CIP

Printed in 11 on 12½ point Plantin Typeface
by Sessions of York
The Ebor Press
York, England

Contents

Illustrations

Author's Note

GENERALLY, THE CHRONOLOGY of John Woolman's *Journal* has been used throughout this work. Some items have not been included and for no other reason than keeping the chain of events flowing and unified as possible. As readers of the *Journal* will know, this has not been an easy task at times.

All quotations not cited in Notes and References are from Phillips P. Moulton's edition of the *Journal*. The author thanks Friends United Press for allowing me to quote from this most recent and authoritative edition of the *Journal*: in itself it is a masterpiece. A primary reason for my writing was to get the reader to enter Woolman's *Journal* and world. I only hope that I may have facilitated this.

It is important to remember that a journal such as Woolman's, and other Quakers, was neither a day-to-day diary nor an autobiography. It is a religious document, a journal of religious development. As John Woolman himself said at the outset he was 'writing of my experience of the goodness of God'.

The reader might be interested in knowing that I am an American writing in England. I have lived here for a quarter of a century and perhaps this experience is fruitful in dealing with one who also was born in America but died in England. For many years – more than I want to recall – I taught American history among other subjects on both sides of the Atlantic.

Thanks are in order for several souls: in Mount Holly, Woolman's hometown, John and Carol Walz at the John Woolman Memorial and to Mary Smith and Edith Ellis.

I also remember the goodly services of the Library of Friends House, London, and the London Library: two truly remarkable institutions. Sylvia Payne was one who first shared an interest in Woolman, and Anne Adams of Quaker Green Concern supplied me with information and inspiration I otherwise would have not known. I also thank Howard Gregg for many acts of kindness and advice. Lastly – to William K. Sessions, the one who made it all possible. After writing seven books over the years and at times dealing with impossible literary agents and editors, I can say that this experience with John Woolman has been the most pleasurable I have known in putting pen to paper.

Rancocas Creek, near Mount Holly.

Introduction

GRACE CATHEDRAL SITS proudly on Nob Hill in San Francisco; albeit humiliated at its east end by an outrageously towering block of flats. After the 1906 earthquake when old Grace Church was destroyed, plans started for a cathedral in the West with a spire which could be seen by ships entering the Golden Gate. However, work for the Gothic edifice in reinforced concrete did not begin until 1928.

The design was said to be inspired by French cathedrals such as Amiens and Chartres but from the beginning modern American features were incorporated including stained glass celebrating – as time went by – American heroes from John Dewey, Luther Burbank, Jane Addams to John Glenn. And in the 'Social Reform' window was a Quaker, a Quaker on horseback no less: John Woolman. A Quaker in stained glass in a Gothic cathedral – that in itself was wonderfully unique – but when I was a minor canon at Grace Cathedral (1970-74) I was often asked just who this particular social reformer was. Not once did I encounter a soul who already knew.

Woolman also appeared in stained glass in Minneapolis in 1967 at the Plymouth Congregational Church, but this was largely due to the pastor, Howard Cann who was a long-time member of the Wider Quaker Fellowship. At Boston University's Muelder Chapel Woolman is again in stained glass, and this time alongside other 'outstanding Christian mystics': John of Damascus, Bernard of Clairvaux and Teresa of Avila. Stained glass attention notwithstanding Woolman remains a less celebrated mystic and social reformer.

This is despite some extraordinary adulation. Harvard Divinity School's Dean Willard Sperry once said of him: 'If I were asked to

1

date the birth of social conscience in its present-day form, I think I should put it on the twenty-sixth day of the eighth month of the year 1758 – the day John Woolman in a public meeting verbally denounced Negro slavery.'[1]

Over the years the accolades for Woolman have been generous and varied: mystic *and* activist, prophet and saint, *schöne seele* (beautiful soul), a perfect exemplar of Quaker empiricism. Ralph Waldo Emerson said of Woolman's *Journal* that he found 'more wisdom in these pages than in any book written since the days of the apostles' and Charles Lamb said it was 'the only American book' he had ever read twice. Lamb advised: 'Get the writings of Woolman by heart' and Coleridge despaired of the man 'who could peruse the life of John Woolman without an amelioration of heart.'[2]

More recently Phillips Moulton went further by claiming that Woolman 'deserves to be ranked among the great spiritual leaders of mankind ... comparable to such better known figures as Albert Schweitzer and Mahatma Gandhi.'[3]

So why isn't John Woolman better known? In the heat of the 1960s civil rights discussion in America Edwin Cady remarked that 'for all the obvious intellectual culture of both, neither (Martin Luther) King nor (James) Baldwin seems aware of the existence of Woolman.'[4]

Why? Part of the reason undoubtedly is due to Woolman's being a Quaker, people not known for sounding their own trumpet, or as Seidel Canby put it: 'Advertising is not a Quaker gift ... the Quaker influence upon the American mind, though diffuse and mingled is far greater than critics and historians have let us suppose.'[5]

This Quaker reserve is also why a biography of Woolman will always be limited. Woolman was extraordinarily self-effacing: he produced three versions of his *Journal* in an effort to eliminate as much as possible the pronoun 'I'.Only on limited occasion do we glimpse Woolman as a son, a father and a husband. He was quiet about himself, his family and his friends, but as we will see the veil is partially lifted through the eyes of others, and their opinions of the man. Also with a careful reading between the lines of his illustrious writing, something of his personality gradually emerges.

2

This volume is not a critical analysis or interpretation of Woolman's *Journal*: that has already been expertly accomplished by others. What is aimed for is an appreciation of a singularly remarkable life and its message for us today. It is hoped that this introduction to Woolman will appeal to a larger audience not likely to tackle the *Journal* unaided. Ultimately the goal is Lamb's injunction to 'get the writings of John Woolman by heart.'

To understand better the man and to recognize just how far ahead of his time he was, it is important to place him into the historical context of 18th-century America: only then will shine forth more clearly Woolman's feelings about slavery, the treatment of North American Indians, his tenderness toward all creatures, his remarkably ethical consumption, warnings about wealth and his irenical attitude regarding other religious expressions.

PART ONE

On the Banks of the Rancocas

IN AMERICAN TRADITION Pennsylvania remains the Quaker state: indeed as a boy I remember a motor oil by that name. Most American school children have heard about William Penn and the Indians; some even learn about the Holy Experiment. Those in Philadelphia know that until 1984 no building in their city was allowed to be taller than the gigantic statue of Penn atop City Hall. But precious few in neighbouring New Jersey know that once it was also a Quaker colony with more than half of the early settlers of that persuasion.

Unlike the fairly straightforward presentation of property by Charles II for the tract which became Penn's Woods, New Jersey became Quaker in a more convoluted manner. In 1664, the Duke of York granted the land between the Hudson and Delaware rivers to Sir George Carteret and Lord John Berkeley. The area was named for Carteret's native island of Jersey. In 1674, Berkeley sold his share to a Quaker whose business affairs became so burdened that the management of the area passed to three trustees, one of whom was William Penn. In 1676, the colony was divided into East and West Jersey with Carteret in control of the east. He sold out in 1682 to a group of twelve; again one of these was William Penn. Soon the earlier Dutch and Swedish settlers were outnumbered by English Quakers, and their number was augmented by Penn's 1677 visit to Germany where he encouraged religious groups similar to the Quakers to come to America.

A year later a shipload of well-to-do settlers arrived on the banks of the Rancocas Creek, a tributary of the Delaware River. They settled in what became Burlington and Mount Holly. Most of them were Quakers and one, John Woolman, was the grandfather of our John Woolman.

Quakerism was among the most radical explosions of 17th-century England; Fox and his followers took the Reformation to what they considered its logical conclusion: no creeds, no set liturgy, no sacraments, not even Baptism or Communion. They believed that man had direct access to God – even the Bible was subject to that Spirit of God which was in every man.

The name – the Religious Society of Friends – indicated the approach: Quakerism was a practical mysticism. As Gerald Priestland has put it: 'a contemplative order within the one great Church that encompasses all Christians.'[6] As will soon be apparent that description would have appealed to John Woolman.

It is said that the Quakers got their appellation from Justice Bennett in 1650 when George Fox bade him tremble (quake) at the Word of God. However, Quakers never quaked like the Shakers shook!

To the established church as well as the Non-conformists, at their inception Quakers were anathema. One American Puritan maintained that the Friends were 'the Devil's agents consulting in mischievous silence the heretic known as the conscience.' He went further: 'If they beat the gospel black and blue, it is just to beat them black and blue.'[7] The Bunhill Fields burial ground in London indicates that ostracism was carried even to the grave. In the unconsecrated grounds were the Non-conformists (among them John Bunyan and William Blake). George Fox, however, and other Quakers were across the road; kept separate even from the Separatists.

John Woolman has been described as 'the purest and sweetest flowering of the Quaker spirit',[8] and most assuredly he can only be appreciated within that background. Every indication points to a childhood imbued with Quaker values. Born 19 October 1720, he was the fourth child and eldest son in a family of thirteen; his early years were dominated by females: as well as his mother, three older sisters and two aunts were in the household.

In such a large family it was only natural that John's eldest sister, Elizabeth, was often in charge of her brother. She was five years older than he, and in the years which followed, the two were extremely close. Elizabeth was the only sibling to whom he referred by name in his *Journal,* and she never married. When she died of the dreadful smallpox in 1747 (she was only 31), John Woolman was devastated. It can be supposed that much of his gentle spirit came from Elizabeth.

The Woolman homestead, on the banks of Rancocas Creek was halfway between Burlington and Mount Holly, and about 18 miles from Philadelphia. It was inherited by Samuel Woolman and consisted of a substantial brick house and a large farm; the Woolmans were neither poor nor particularly well-to-do. A mile away was the little schoolhouse where for ten years young John had his formal education. Undoubtedly he learned a great deal at home where his father had a good-sized library; the Woolmans also had access to fine book collections of wealthy friends in Philadelphia. Throughout his life John took advantage of that connection. At home the Bible and other religious books were read each First Day. Though he was not especially intellectual, Samuel Woolman recognized that his eldest son required more than usual cerebral stimulation.

Of his father Woolman said:

In his lifetime he manifested much care for us his children, that in our youth we might learn to fear the Lord, and often endeavoured to imprint in our minds the true principles of virtue, and particularly to cherish in us a spirit of tenderness, not only towards poor people, but also towards all creatures, of which we had the command.

John's mother, Elizabeth Burr, came from a substantial family. Her father Henry could not read or write but began to purchase land in Burlington County in 1680. By 1714, he had amassed a thousand acres. In 1695, he bought Peachfield the attractive plantation which was carefully rebuilt in 1931 and remains today a memorial to the Burr family. It is an irony that Henry's grandson-in-law, John Woolman, was one of the first antislavery agitators while his great, great, great granddaughter married Jefferson Davis, the President of the Confederate States of America.

Familial incongruity was earlier as well: Woolman's first cousin, Timothy Matlock, Jr. (son of one of Elizabeth Woolman's sisters) actively espoused the colonists' cause during the War for American

6

Independence and helped form the Free (Fighting) Quakers, those who abandoned Quaker pacifism in the war. Much to the chagrin of the Woolmans and like-minded Friends, Matlock often strode the streets of Philadelphia 'garbed in Quaker clothes and with a sword girded around him.'[9] Samuel Woolman died in 1750 when John was only 22, but his mother would outlive him by a year.

Woolman said he was 'taught to read near as I was capable of it' and his writing clearly indicates a wide exposure to books. Edwin Cady has made much of this point and takes to task those Woolman commentators who 'underscored the paradox of his writing's having come from an "illiterate", "unlearned", poverty-stricken "tailor" or "shop-keeper"'.[10] It was not until Woolman was 36 that he started writing his *Journal*, but in a list of twenty-eight 'books lent' from his library and recorded in his ledger we see a wide reading spectrum. As expected, the bulk of the works were Quaker classics like Fox's *Book of Doctrinals*, Barclay's *Apology*, Sewel's *History* and Penn's *No Cross No Crown*.

There were also Quaker journals (religious autobiographies we might call them) which would affect the style for his own *Journal*. In the ledger were some surprises as well: books on navigation, cider making, Indian treaties and John Locke's brilliant *Some Thoughts Concerning Education* which was just becoming popular among sophisticated readers in the colonies.

Woolman's *Journal* is peppered with references from mystic tradition including *Imitation of Christ* attributed to the Catholic Thomas à Kempis – at a time when most Protestants considered Catholics to be akin to the Antichrist. We also see the writings of the mystics Jakob Boehme, John Everard and William Law. Law was an interesting influence: an English churchman who was Woolman's contemporary and studied Jakob Boehme. That led to a larger involvement with mysticism. Law was also influenced by John Wesley, but the two parted company on mysticism as well as Law's stressing the doctrine of the Incarnation rather than the Atonement of Christ. In later life Law was criticized for becoming too much like the Quakers; among other things he was a vigorous believer in the unlawfulness of war.

There are some 700 quotations from Scripture and Cady remarks 'there can be no doubt about John Woolman's command of the Bible ... an intimate familiarity which showed that he *thought* biblically.'[11] As would be understandable for a Quaker he appeared to have a preference for John's Gospel, Isaiah, Jeremiah and passages such as the Golden Rule and Matthew 6:19 ('Lay not up for yourselves treasures upon earth ...').

In the first paragraph of his *Journal* Woolman gave his reason for writing his religious autobiography: 'I have often felt a motion of love to learn some hints in writing of my experience of the goodness of God ...' Woolman said that he was seven years old when he 'began to be acquainted with the operations of divine love,' but gave little from his childhood except for two or three experiences. One was a day after returning from school when as his friends went off to play, John sat down and read from the Bible – the last chapter of the last book no less – Revelation 22: 'And he showed me a pure river of water of life, as crystal ... in the midst ... the tree of life which bare twelve manner of fruits ...' In that reading, Woolman's mind was 'drawn to seek after that pure habitation ... I then believed God had prepared for his servants.' The place where he sat 'and the sweetness that attended my mind' remained fresh in his memory as later he wrote in his *Journal*. Trees, leaves, fruit, a 'pure river' – all imagery important to a boy of the country.

Young Woolman's becoming acquainted with God was a quiet and gentle affair: quite unlike, for example, four-year-old William Blake who said he saw God looking at him through a window which made him scream. Nor was it Luther's youthful vowing to become a monk when he became frightened in a thunderstorm. But a little book published in 1897 on John Woolman 'for young men' by an Anglican clergyman made a useful remark about the young Woolman:

> Life as recorded in the model volumes he read and life as he witnessed it around him, presented points of contrast not favourable to the present, and the reflection caused him, as a child, no little trouble.[12]

His father's admonition for 'a spirit of tenderness ... towards all creatures' was wonderfully perfected in the young John. As will be further noted, John Woolman was singularly unique in his concern for animals; undoubtedly nurtured by an animal-loving father and reinforced by one of the experiences he related from his childhood. Like most boys he thoughtlessly threw stones at a bird and killed it. Then he discovered it was a mother robin (a large russet-breasted thrush) with offspring. John was

> seized with horror, as having in a sportive way killed an inno-
> cent creature while she was careful for her young. I beheld her
> lying dead and thought those young ones for which she so care-
> ful must perish for want of their dam to nourish them; and after
> some painful considerations on the subject, I climbed up the
> tree, took all the young birds and killed them, supposing that
> better than to leave them to pine away and die miserably ...

That experience stayed with John Woolman and soon he became a lover of all creatures; today he is often quoted by animal concern groups much in the manner of St Francis. Like other mystics, Woolman also presents us with a number of dreams in his *Journal*; the first occurred when he was nine years old. In this dream Woolman was standing in the doorway of his father's house and saw the moon rise near the west and travel eastward across the sky. When the moon appeared overhead a small cloud 'on a direct line to the earth' drifted down and settled on the ground and turned into a beautiful green tree. As the moon set in the east the sun began to rise. The heat of the sun withered the tree and 'before noon it appeared dry and dead.' Next Woolman dreamed that 'a being, small of size, full of strength and resolution' moved swiftly from the south. He said it was called 'a sun worm.'

Woolman did not give an interpretation to the dream and Janet Whitney says it was 'a queer dream, so meaningless like some of those dreams in the Bible, and so peculiarly his own.'[13] But she also could not resist adding: 'The boy himself a being small of size, he did in time to come move southward ...'[14] We are left with the simple fact that the dream stayed long in Woolman's memory but its significance remains a mystery.

When John reached twelve years of age, Elizabeth would have been 17, Sarah 15, Patience 14. Next, two brothers, Asher and Abner would have been ten and eight and they were all followed by younger siblings. John must have felt the pressure – and independence – of being the oldest boy in a large family. At that age he says that once when his father was away, his mother reproved him for some misdeed and he 'made an undutiful reply.' When his father returned and they were leaving First Day Meeting, Samuel Woolman told his son that he understood that he had misbehaved. John knew he was to blame and afterwards that he did not remember ever speaking 'unhandsomely to either of my parents, however foolish in other things.' No rod necessary and today we marvel at such respect for parents coming from a twelve-year-old. Barry Levy sheds a general light on the situation in his investigation of Quaker families in the Delaware Valley of the time saying that they

> brought a new vision of family life to America ... one that contrasted sharply with the harsh, formal world of Puritan New England. The Quaker emphasis was on affection, friendship and hospitality. They stressed the importance of women in the home, and of ... noncoercive child-rearing.[15]

Despite his extraordinary self-discipline, young John Woolman was never a 'loner' and appeared to have been popular with his peers. Indeed, by the time he was sixteen, he could say that he 'began to love wanton company,' but he also added that he was 'preserved from profane language or scandalous conduct.'

As he advanced in years the number of John's acquaintances increased and he said that his own 'Way' and that of his friends diverged. Much as with young Francis of Assisi it all came to a crisis when John also became ill and he 'doubted of recovery.' But like Francis he did get better and with 'new resolve' he tried to keep away from 'folly'. Once as he was retiring for the night John picked up a Bible and came across the text from Jeremiah 3.25: 'We lie down in our shame and our confusion covers us.' He knew the words were speaking to him and he went to bed 'under a remorse of conscience.'

In our day psychologists would probably say that such a dutiful boy was being unduly hard on himself. However, for the next few years John vacillated between 'new resolve' and 'turning again to folly.' Then he decided:

I was now led to look seriously at the means by which I was drawn from the pure Truth, and learned this: that if I would live in the life which faithful servants of God lived in, I must not go into company as heretofore in my own will, but all the cravings of sense must be governed by a divine principle ...

Woolman's notion of 'a divine principle' – developed at a tender age – remains one of the purest expressions of Quakerism to be found:

I kept steady to meetings, spent First Days afternoon chiefly in reading the Scriptures and other good books, and was early convinced in my mind that true religion consisted in an inward life, wherein the heart doth love and reverence God the Creator and learn to exercise true justice and goodness, not only toward all men but also toward the brute creatures; that as the mind was moved on an inward principle to love God as an invisible, incomprehensible being, on the same principle it was moved to love him in all his manifestations in the visible world; that as by his breath the flame of life was kindled in all animal and sensitive creatures, to say we love God as unseen and at the same time exercise cruelty toward the least creature moving by his life, or by life derived from him, was a contradiction in itself ...

I found no narrowness respecting sects and opinions, but believed that sincere, upright-hearted people in every Society who truly loved God were accepted of him.

What remarkable ideas from one so young: a divine principle of charity, inward searching, one which put no limit to any particular religious group, and most striking of all (considering the time), God's love extended to all his creatures; even the brute creatures.

Well-honed Conscience

IT WAS NOT LONG until John Woolman began to have difficulties with his well-honed conscience. It occurred – as it does with many – when he started working for a living. Until he was twenty-one, Woolman lived with his parents, and then a local man 'in much business, shopkeeping and baking' asked him if he might be interested in tending a shop and keeping books in Mount Holly. John had received training from his father in book-keeping and legal business. This was at a time when lawyers and accountants were scarce. John Woolman talked the matter over with his father; the offer appeared quite acceptable, but it also brought a great change in his life.

Now Woolman lived alone above a shop and five miles away from what he had always known as home. His employer was also several miles away. Woolman was apprehensive:

> At home I had lived retired, and now having a prospect of being much in the way of company I felt frequent and fervent cries in my heart to God, the Father of all mercies, that he would preserve me from all taint, that in this more public employ I might serve him ... in that humility and self-denial with which I had been in a small degree exercised in a very private life.

Soon there were other difficulties as well. The word spread among his acquaintances that he was in charge of a shop in Mount Holly and they started visiting him; probably hoping that John would join them at the inn just down the street. We have no exact idea of what type of horseplay with which they were involved. But other Quaker journals indicate that it was probably no more than dancing, jesting, card playing and such. However, young John Woolman was convinced that this influence stood between him and his 'way' and so he parted company once and for all with his old acquaintances.

A more brusque intrusion entered John's world with the arrival of several indentured servants purchased by his employer. It is often forgotten just how many arrived in the American colonies in this manner, but the migrate-now-and-pay-later system was essential in populating America. Many Highland Scots and those who came to be called Scots-Irish (or more often in America, Scotch-Irish) arrived in Philadelphia in this manner. As one historian says, 'Scotch-Irish is an enduring misnomer for Ulster Scots Presbyterians transplanted from Scotland to confiscated lands in northern Ireland to give the country a more Protestant tone.'[16] Renowned for their piety it was said the Scotch-Irish 'kept the Sabbath and everything else they could lay their hands on.'[17] Quakers especially found them troublesome as they harboured an abiding hatred for the Indians with whom the Friends early developed good relations. Those hired by Woolman's employer were brought to his shop in Mount Holly until they could find new masters.

Undoubtedly they were big, rough and uncouth – as well as eager to start working out their indentures. One can only imagine the impression they made upon Woolman – and he on them. They were accommodated in his own chamber and when there was only one left to be sold he became seriously ill: 'he, being delirious, used to curse and swear most sorrowfully.' He died and was buried and Woolman was 'left to sleep alone the next night in the same chamber where he did.' Woolman admitted to feeling timorous, but knew that he 'had not injured the man but assisted in taking care of him according to my capacity ...'

Woolman was very regular at Meetings and early started to 'minister'. For non-Quakers that needs explaining. There were no paid ministers, no ordained clergy in the Society of Friends and any Quaker – male or female – was free to 'minister' at Meeting: vocally expressing feelings coming in the gathered meeting for worship. During Woolman's time it was customary to record those with vocal gifts as 'Ministers'; subsequently the name was changed to elders. These recorded ministers gave a type of pastoral leadership and often visited other meetings up and down the east coast.

Of his initial ministry at meeting Woolman wrote: 'I stood up and said some words in a Meeting, but not keeping close to the divine opening I said more than was required.' Beatrice Snell has commented: 'Characteristically he meditated on the cause of his apparent failure.'[18] Being sensible to his error, Woolman was 'afflicted' in his mind 'for some weeks without any light or comfort.' In fact Woolman did not speak again at meeting for about six weeks until his

> understanding became more strengthened to distinguish the language of the pure Spirit inwardly move upon the heart and taught (me) to wait in silence ... until I felt that rise which prepares the creature to stand like a trumpet which the Lord speaks to his flock.

After two years of employment Woolman felt: 'In the management of my outward affairs I may say with thankfulness I found Truth to be my support.' Now he was twenty-three and his employer's family came to live in Mount Holly; it was then he faced the first great crisis of conscience – and set the future course of his life.

It all started when his employer decided to sell a female black slave. One of Woolman's duties was, of course, legal work so he was asked to write the bill of sale. Woolman was perplexed: 'the thought of writing an instrument of slavery for one of my fellow creatures felt uneasy ...' Woolman was told that she was being purchased by a Quaker but that did not ease his mind. He had to speak out to his boss and said that he thought slave-keeping was 'a practice inconsistent with the Christian religion.'

In his *Journal* he reflected that speaking up like that 'abated' his 'uneasiness' to a degree, but later when he thought more about it, he wished that he had been 'clearer' with his employer at the time. Anyhow, the experience prepared him for the future. Sometime afterward when a young Quaker asked him to write another bill of sale for a slave he responded that he 'was not easy' to do it. The young man admitted that keeping slaves was not 'altogether agreeable' to him, but as the slave in question had been a gift to his wife, he had accepted the situation.

Thus began John Woolman's singular crusade against slavery: a slow but steady pricking of consciences within the Society of Friends. That would – in time – lead to the abolition of the

14

practice altogether among Quakers and gradually from them the opening up of the debate among many others in America.

Quaker Meeting House, Burlington, New Jersey
Built about 1680 and in existence for nearly a hundred years.
From a drawing printed on page 53 of Hubert Lidbetter's
The Friends Meeting House.

The Institution of Slavery

THE INSTITUTION OF slavery appears almost incomprehensible today; how could those who call themselves Christian ever have been involved in the buying and selling of human beings? Shipped in appalling conditions from one continent to another; families were separated and those purchased faced lives picking cotton, indigo and tobacco. The motive was in the cheap production of those plants and it was a strong motive: greed. Fortunes were to be made but large numbers of labourers were required in the fields. It all started earlier than many suppose: by 1619, tobacco production had already reached 20,000 pounds in Virginia, and by the time Woolman made his first journey south, South Carolina shipped more than a million pounds of indigo to England.

But less than five per cent of the black labour force brought from Africa went to British North-America – 400,000 out of 9,500,000. The rest went to the Indies and Latin America. And as Alistair Cooke comments:

> To the Portuguese goes the melancholy privilege of having started the European enslavement of African Negroes ... it was systematized under the Kings of Spain to 'lighten' the burdens of the natives of the West Indies.[19]

But it wasn't just Latin American and the Southern English colonists who profited: Yankee shipbuilders made fortunes out of the trade. Blacks regularly arrived in Northern as well as Southern ports. Ironically the first were in a ship named *Jesus of Lubeck*, only twelve years after Jamestown was founded. In time almost everyone of substance had Negro servants, Quakers among them. Edwin Cady reminds us,

Seventeenth-century colonists were accustomed to bound apprentices, indentured servants, transported criminals, and whites as well as Indians sold into slavery for political or other reasons. As Quakers had ample reason to know, it was a callous age throughout the world.[20]

But the practice was questioned early in Quaker history. In 1657 George Fox wrote 'To Friends Beyond Sea that Have Blacks and Indian Slaves' to caution them to the mercifulness of Christ and the necessity to display kindness 'to every captivated creature under the whole heaven.' Fox preached to slaves in Barbados in 1671 and urged slaveholders to set an indenture-like term to their servitude. In 1688 Germantown Quakers at their monthly meeting asked some embarrassing questions: Could slavery fulfill the Golden Rule? Was it not a complex of crimes? How could it be reconciled with Quaker testimonies of love, peace, liberty and non-violence?

As we will see, Benjamin Lay also raised his prophetic voice and Joseph Arnold, a Rhode Island Quaker, refused to stay in inns or homes owned by Quaker slaveholders when he went to Newport Yearly Meeting in 1745. The time was right for further action and it would be within his own religious house that Woolman would campaign.

This was largely accomplished through Woolman's journeys – 'travelling in the Ministry' as it was known. In 1746 (when he was twenty-six), in a three-month period, Woolman covered 1,500 miles by foot and on horseback. The stained glass image of him in Grace Cathedral presents him on a horse, but his latter-day trips were almost always on foot.

The first of the journeys occurred when Abraham Farrington, a real estate agent in Philadelphia, planned to visit the eastern shore of New Jersey. Having no companion Farrington asked Woolman to accompany him. Their first stop was in Brunswick in which Woolman noted 'none of our Society dwells.' Later they were at Woodbridge, Rahway and Plainfield 'where Friends' meetings are not usually held, being made up chiefly of Presbyterians.' That did not deter either from joining them in worship and Woolman said that Farrington was 'frequently strengthened to hold forth the Word of Life amongst them.' Woolman himself usually remained silent but he added: 'My mind was often tender and I learned some profitable lessons.'

After several years in employment Woolman began to question where it was leading. He received 'several offers of business that appeared profitable' but that didn't please him: 'the business proposal would be attended with more outward care and cumber.' That delightful word cumber was a favourite of Woolman, but there was more in his usage of it than the present dictionary meaning of 'hindrance, obstraction.'

Cumber stood in the way of what Woolman demanded from himself and where his heart was moving; he was beginning to see that

> a humble man with the blessing of the Lord might live on a little, and that where the heart was set on greatness, success in business did not satisfy the craving, but that in common with an increase of wealth the desire of wealth increased.

Oh how far we have come from that simple truth: try presenting that conviction in today's market.

John Woolman: tailor.
Reproduced from Janet Whitney's John Woolman Quaker.

Woolman looked in other directions. His employer was a tailor by trade and that line of occupation appealed to him: 'I might ... get a living in a plain way without the load of great business.' His employer agreed to his terms and Woolman became the tailor of Mount Holly: 'I had seen the happiness of humility and there was an earnest desire in me to enter deep into it.'

Not long after this, his employer's wife died and he left shop-keeping. Now Woolman was completely on his own as an independent tailor. With less cumber, he embarked on his first journey south, and it would affect him greatly. Isaac Andrews, a close neighbour in Mount Holly, accompanied him. Like Woolman Andrews felt 'drawn' to visit Maryland, Virginia and North Carolina. This, of course, was not the 'Deep South' and it would be interesting to know how Woolman would have reacted facing the fuller operation of slavery as in South Carolina and Georgia. But there were hardly any Quaker families that far south. Travelling as the two did with certificates from the Monthly Meeting opened the necessary doors as Quakers were expected to offer hospitality to any members of the Society.

Woolman said they were soon 'baptized' into sensing the conditions of the people they encountered. Phillips Moulton observes that 'baptized' meant initiated, made aware; 'generally implying that the awareness (was) brought about through a trying experience.'[21] Woolman certainly was troubled with the ease with which the Southerners lived 'on the hard labour of their slaves.'

In cases where the masters lived frugally and carried much of the work themselves, ensuring that the slaves were well provided for, Woolman 'felt more easy.' But where the masters had a more extravagant lifestyle based on 'heavy burdens on their slaves' he was deeply troubled.

Woolman went further in his observations: to him 'a dark gloominess' was 'hanging on the land; and though now many willingly run into it, yet in the future the consequences will be grievous to posterity.' At the time Woolman had no idea how far-sighted and prophetic that remark was: in another hundred years the American nation would split in two over the evil institution.

New England and Marriage

THE YEAR FOLLOWING his first journey south, Woolman's sister, Elizabeth, died of smallpox. In his *Journal* he remembered her (the only sibling he so commemorated) as living 'a self-denying, exemplary life, giving herself much to reading and meditation.' Her illness must have been excruciating: the first symptoms were headache, loss of appetite and rising temperature. Even after the ugly red rash first appeared it was possible Elizabeth had measles or scarlet fever. But when the red lumps began to surface at the roots of her hair the family knew it was the horrible smallpox which had taken so many others in the area. Despite the considerable suffering known to accompany the disease, Elizabeth was singularly composed. One friend who came some distance to see Elizabeth the morning before she died asked her how she remained so brave. Elizabeth remarked that she had had a difficult night but that there would not be another 'for I shall die, and it will be well with my soul.' She was right: shortly after saying this Elizabeth Woolman was dead.

Her will indicated a well-ordered life in another respect. There was money left for her six brothers and four sisters. Her household effects went to Hannah, and Patience got her best gowns. To her father she willed her great Bible, a looking glass for her mother – and to her beloved John: the sum of £12.00 and ironically some gold buttons!

In 1747 Woolman said that he had 'drawings' in his mind to visit New England. For him the word meant something between guidance and mission. It was an interesting time to be drawn to New England as America's 'first mass movement' (the Great Awakening) had been fermenting for over a decade. It all started at Jonathan Edwards' church in Northampton, Massachusetts.

Edwards, a Congregationalist minister thought that New England religion had turned cold and depressing: 'Our people do not so much need to have their heads stored as to have their hearts touched.' Edwards certainly touched their hearts, and with the reality of hell: 'Sinners in the hands of an angry God: God holds you over the pit of hell, much as one holds a spider, or some loathsome insect, over the fire, abhors you, and is dreadfully provoked ...'[22]

Well, Edwards certainly shook the staid Puritan establishment to its foundations and his and other revivalism brought 25,000 to 50,000 New Englanders (out of a population of 300,000) into churches. These new recruits were dubbed 'New Lights'; many of them became Presbyterians and Baptists. But it would be the Methodists who benefited most from the waves of revival which swept through the colonies.

A major reason for this was that the true catalyst of the Great Awakening was not Edwards but the twenty-seven-year-old English Methodist, George Whitefield. After pulpits were denied to Whitefield in England, he followed Wesley to Georgia and was appointed minister at Savannah. He was a brilliant preacher, impressing Edwards so much that he openly wept through one of Whitefield's sermons. But Whitefield had his differences with Wesley: Whitefield stayed a rigid Calvinist upholding predestination in the manner of the Puritans. There was no doubt, however, about the popularity of Whitefield's revivals; at one in Philadelphia even the sceptical Benjamin Franklin was so carried away with the emotionalism that he emptied his pockets into the collection plate.

Whitefield gave enormous impetus to the growth of Methodism and it would, in time, become the most popular American denomination. It remained so until our own day when Methodists were outdistanced in numbers by the Southern Baptists. Methodists and Baptists who vacillated when it came to the slavery issue flourished especially in the South. But as Jack Marietta writes: 'Individual Friends would not be allowed to ignore Quaker abolitionist strictures as Southern Methodists ignored the orders of their General Conference.'[23] The force of revivalism, however, passed the Quakers by and their numbers remained forever small – especially in the South.

It comes as a surprise to learn that, according to Edwin Gaustad's recent calculations, in 1750 the Quakers were the third largest religious body in British North America – outnumbered only by the Congregationalists and the Anglicans. In a hundred years time (1850) the Quakers had dropped to eighth position and in another hundred years, the Society of Friends was one of America's many minor sects. But as Marietta well says: 'Friends did not define the prosperity of Christianity in an evangelical or democratic way ... As the Society of Friends gravitated away from the center of American society, it became a sanctuary for odd, holy men and women'[24] – a position from which it had started in England in the 17th-century.

An interesting side effect of some of the revivalism was that some 'New Lights' began to question the issue of slavery, but unfortunately it would only be much later that abolitionism took root in Methodism and other denominations. Whitefield himself spoke of the 'miseries of the poor negroes' and was 'sure it was sinful' but when it came to the principle of slavery itself, he hedged: 'Whether it be lawful for Christians to buy slaves ... I shall not take upon me to determine.'[25]

Shortly after that pronouncement Whitefield felt it necessary to use slaves himself, and at the Methodist orphanage in Savannah no less. Slavery was destined to become an issue which like the nation itself, would split the church into Northern and Southern segments. Black Methodists themselves were to have their own separate denominations.

In 1747, as the Great Awakening was subsiding and fragmenting in the old Puritan heartland, Woolman joined his 'beloved friend' Peter Andrews who was also 'travelling in the ministry'. First they attended Yearly Meeting on Long Island and then they went on to Setauket and Oyster Bay. Woolman called these areas the 'back settlements' and indeed they were at that time. There they encountered young people who were holding their own meetings. Apparently they had been affected by the revivalism which had even reached these parts and it seems at first that their Presbyterian preacher appeared to approve. But later he detected deviations from orthodox Calvinism among them. The boys were rebuked but some of them were further attracted to Quakerism. Woolman talked extensively with these 'New Lights' and believed they were well acquainted with 'the nature of that worship which is performed in spirit and in Truth.' But as always Woolman refrained from proselytizing among them.

Joined by Amos Powell, a Quaker bachelor from Long Island, Woolman and Andrews travelled on to Connecticut which Woolman described as 'chiefly inhabited by Presbyterians.' Like others of his time 'Presbyterian' was employed to encompass a variety of Calvinist-based sects. The Connecticut 'Presbyterians' were, of course, as with their comrades in Massachusetts, successors to the Puritans and were by this time generally calling themselves Congregationalists.

The first Quakers to arrive in New England had been Mary Fisher and Ann Austin; that was in Boston in 1656. Almost immediately they were imprisoned. After eleven weeks in jail the two women were exiled but other Quakers followed – and were suppressed. Four of them faced martyrdom. It would take some time for Quakers to be accepted in the land of the Pilgrims.

By the time John Woolman made his first visit he found the inhabitants 'generally civil to us as far as I saw'. From Newport they sailed to Nantucket where Quakers had settled by the beginning of the 18th-century. Several meeting houses were built and the largest on Pleasant and Main Streets came to accommodate 1,500 people. By 1762, the Quaker community had grown to 2,400. Part of their success was due to their involvement in the whaling industry about which Woolman made no remarks until his second visit to the island.

Crime was almost absent from Nantucket making police and justices idle. There were also good relations with the Algonquian Indians and early Nantucket Quakers played a role towards the abolition of slavery. In November 1716 it was recorded in the minutes of their meeting that slavery was 'not agreeable to Friends'.

Generally Woolman had mixed feelings about his first visit to New England. As we will later note, Newport was extremely involved with the slave trade and Quakers were among those profiting from it. Woolman said that he and Peter Andrews 'were sometimes in much discouragements' but 'at other times' they had 'seasons of refreshment wherein the power of Truth prevailed.' However, Woolman had no equivocation concerning his companion, Peter Andrews: 'He was about thirteen years older than I, bore the heaviest burden, and was an instrument of the greatest use.'

John Woolman waited until he was 29 to get married and again we receive few details from his own lips. What he did relate is unguardedly charming:

> About this time believing it good for me to settle and thinking seriously about a companion, my heart turned to the Lord ... and he was pleased to give me a well-inclined damsel, Sarah Ellis.

Sometimes we read that Sarah was called 'cousin' by the Woolman family, but she was not related by blood. However, as most of her life was spent within a few miles of Mount Holly, she shared friends and relations with the Woolmans. Apparently shortly after her birth, Sarah's father was lost at sea; her mother died eleven years before Sarah married John Woolman. Sarah was never in the best of health, but she did survive her husband by fifteen years. Their first child, Mary, was born in the first year of their marriage; four years later they had a son but he lived only a month or two. That delivery was so difficult that Sarah was unable to have any more children.

The year after his marriage (1750) John Woolman's father died. Woolman said that one night during his father's illness he watched his father, realizing that he was not going to get better. His father asked about a manuscript his son had written and whether he expected to offer it to the Quaker Overseers of the Press. Then his father told John: 'I have all along been deeply affected with the oppression of poor Negroes, and now at last my concern for them is as great as ever.'

The manuscript John's father mentioned was *Some Considerations on the Keeping of Negroes* which basically was the fruit of Woolman's 1746 journey to the South. It was not published until seven years later, but Philadelphia Yearly Meeting had it printed and distributed at its own expense. The overseers distributed the tract to every Yearly Meeting in America and sent copies to England. The historian Thomas Drake wrote:

No other antislavery document had hitherto received such extensive circulation in any language anywhere. It opened the way and set the pattern for pamphlets by Anthony Benezet on Africa and the slave trade, for pamphleting by John Wesley, Granville Sharpe and Thomas Clarkson in England and for antislavery pronouncements by Philadelphia Yearly Meeting.[26]

Nowhere in the essay did Woolman mention the Society of Friends specifically: it was addressed to 'Professors of Christianity of every Denomination,' meaning those who 'professed' the Christian faith. One would have to be very callous not to be moved by Woolman's calm and modest tone. He said that his inclination was 'to persuade and entreat, and simply give hints of my way of thinking.'

From the beginning Woolman insisted that 'in considering slavery it would be the highest wisdom to forego customs and popular opinions, and try the treasures of the soul by the infallible standard: Truth.' Truth was where to begin and by Truth Woolman meant 'Ultimate spiritual reality; divinity' as distinguished from particular truths such as credal affirmations.

In words later used by some abolitionists, Woolman reminded his readers that

all natures are of one blood (Genesis 3.20); that in this world we are but sojourners; that we are subject to the like afflictions and infirmities of body, the like disorders and frailties in mind, the like temptations, the same death and the same judgment; and the All-wise Being is judge and Lord over us all ...

But Woolman never resorted to the fiery judgments later found in abolitionism. The nearest he came to that emotion was: 'To consider mankind otherwise than brethren, to think favours are peculiar to one nation and exclude others, plainly supposes a darkness in the understanding.' Gently Woolman asked for one man

not to look upon another man or society of men as so far beneath him that he should put himself into their place in all his actions towards them and bring them to this test, viz: How should I

25

approve of this conduct were I in their circumstances and they in mine?'

The year before the essay was published (1754) Woolman was visited by the brother of a man who was quite ill and wanted his will executed. Woolman knew the man and that he had slaves he intended to leave to his children. Woolman had well learned from past experience, and before the brother got very far into the matter, Woolman told him that he 'had a scruple in mind against doing writings of that kind.'

The brother 'made no reply to what I said' wrote Woolman and just went away. Woolman knew that he was displeased with him and taking such stands bothered him: 'Offending people is disagreeable to my inclination.' But John Woolman also felt that acting from 'a motive of divine love and in regard to truth ... opens the way to a treasure better than silver, and to a friendship exceeding the friendship of men.'

See earlier: page 23.

Part of a Quaker tapestry panel, as reproduced in colour in Separation from the World, *edited by Jeanne H. Louis of France.*

26

Dreams and War

A S WE HAVE SEEN, John Woolman is, on occasion, referred to as a mystic, but like Rufus Jones, of a decidedly practical nature; a flavouring away from great Church mystics such as John of Damascus, Catherine of Siena or Teresa of Avila. For example, Woolman could never have been portrayed as Bernini presented Teresa in the throes of ecstatic vision with an angel thrusting a long golden dart through her heart.

More than even the Puritans, the early Quakers obliterated any vestiges of superstition from religious practice. There was to be no consultation with soothsayers or necromancers. Witchcraft was unheard of in the Quaker colonies, and consequently there was a considerable reticence to give much credence to the interpretation of dreams and visions. Nevertheless as Howard Brinton has written: 'many dreams are recorded in the vast sum of Quaker religious autobiography.'[27]

There were George Fox's visions of a great people to be gathered or an ocean of darkness and an ocean of light. Woolman's dreams were of a different order and Sterling Olmsted says that 'the absence of such visions is what makes Woolman so accessible to many of us.'[28]

Interestingly, the original editors of the two most widely read Quaker journals – those of Fox and Woolman – omitted nearly all the dreams. It is only latter-day that we have come to appreciate them for what they are.

The second recorded dream in Woolman's *Journal* occurred, as he said, 'on the 7th day, 2nd month, 1754 at night,' and he was 'walking in an orchard.' Unlike the earlier childhood dream the meaning of this one became fairly clear. There were two lights in

27

the east 'resembling two suns, but of a dull and gloomy aspect.' Soon the air in the east 'appeared to be mingled of fire' and it reached the orchard where Woolman stood in his dream. He 'felt no harm', but discovered that a companion standing next to him was 'greatly distressed.'

But even in this potentially troublesome dreaming, Woolman remained characteristically calm telling his friend: 'We must all once die, and if it please the Lord that our death be in this way, it is good for us to be resigned.' Next Woolman entered a house and 'going upstairs saw people with sad and troubled aspects.' He passed into another room and out of a window saw

> three great red streams standing at equal distance from each other, the bottom of which appeared to stand on the earth and the top to reach above the region of the clouds. Across those three streams went less ones, and from each end of such small stream others extended in regular lines to the earth, all red and appeared to extend through the whole southern firmament.

If up to this point the reader of his *Journal* had no idea as to what was occurring, that which followed made it clear: '(appearing) on a green plain' were

> a great multitude of men in a military posture some of whom I knew. They came near the house, and passing on westward some of them, looking up at me, expressed themselves in a scoffing, taunting way, to which I made no reply; soon after, an old captain of the militia came to me, and I was told these men were assembled to improve in the discipline of war.

Coming as it did on the eve of the French and Indian War (1754-1763), the dream appears prophetic and has been called a 'prevision of that war'. But as Amelia Gummere rightly remarks 'that is claiming too much.'[29] Woolman would have been distinctly uncomfortable being presented in the role of soothsayer and he recorded the dream without comment.

Americans knew the Seven Years War as the French and Indian War, and in a sense, it was a continuation of four European and inter-colonial conflicts over a period of sixty-four years. The battles in America were but a sideshow to the European power plays, and a climatic conflict between Britain and France. By this time, the French controlled the valleys of the Mississippi, Ohio and St Lawrence rivers and the British colonies were sprinkled along the Atlantic seaboard from the border of Spanish Florida northwards to the mouth of the St Lawrence.

The outbreak of conflict in America started when adventurous Virginians crossed the Appalachian mountains into the upper Ohio Valley to look over the 200,000 acres given by King George and to begin trading with the local Indians. This enraged the French who interpreted the action as intrusion into their territory. They reacted by building a series of forts in the area and clashes between the British and French soon occurred. Sadly Indian tribes friendly to the French were pitted against those supporting the British. Many were caught right in the middle, and most tribes correctly saw the war as of no profit to them. They tried to stay neutral but that became impossible.

With their traditional pacifism plus friendly relations with the Indians, Quakers were the majority in the Pennsylvania Assembly (28 of the 36 members were Quaker). It was not long before the Quakers were isolated from other colonists who insisted that it was their duty to support the British government and the tax levied to carry on the war. It was this issue which brought seventy-four years of Quaker government in Pennsylvania to an end. When General Edward Braddock's army was defeated at Fort Dusquesne in western Pennsylvania, the exasperated Indians were let loose on the frontiers. The Governor and his council (the Quaker member alone dissenting) declared war against the Delaware and Shawnee Indians, and Friends resigned their places in the Assembly. Within a year, decades of good will toward the Native Americans collapsed.

As will later be explored, the Proprietory government (the successors to William Penn) and the Quaker-dominated Assembly had manoeuvred against each other throughout the 1750s. A figure not often mentioned in these politics was the Reverend William Smith who, Jack Marietta says, 'dealt a blow to both the Quaker politicians and the whole of the Society of Friends as well.'[30] Like other Anglicans involved in the early history of the American Episcopal Church, Smith was a Scottish Episcopalian and the first provost of the College of Philadelphia. Early in 1755, Smith anonymously presented an unsavoury pamphlet entitled *A Brief State of the*

29

Province of Pennsylvania in which he blamed the Quakers and their German compatriots (Moravians, Brethren and Mennonites) for France's success in western Pennsylvania. Smith ranted against the Germans as 'ignorant, proud, stubborn clowns'. What the Quakers and Germans had in common was, of course, that they were pacifists and friendly to the Indians. This combination would never defend Pennsylvania. Smith suggested a devious way out of the Quaker dominance in the Assembly: make them swear oaths of allegiance which was, of course, against their principles. He also said that the Germans should remain disenfranchised until they became 'educated'. Some Scotch-Irish Presbyterians as well as Anglicans took note of Smith's pamphlet but informed and neutral Pennsylvanians saw it as grossly partisan. Anyhow, by the next year – 1756 – the Quakers had withdrawn from government.

There were Quakers who compromised on the issue of paying the war tax and some young Quakers joined the militia, but as expected, John Woolman refused to compromise saying: 'To conform a little to a wrong way strengthens the hands of such who carry customs to their utmost extent.' As Beatrice Saxon Snell well commented: 'Yet if he were the only man in the Society to stand by the principle of no contributions to the war-effort, stand by it he would.'[31]

Two months after General Braddock's defeat, Quakers made their way toward Yearly Meeting in Philadelphia. Earlier John Woolman had written that it was Quaker 'duty to cease from those national contests productive of misery and bloodshed.' But now he was not alone and with thirteen others he signed an epistle presenting the case for refusing to pay taxes levied to support the war.

Quaker objection to the payment of taxes for military purposes, therefore, has had a long history. In the Revolution, American Quakers followed Woolman's example, and during the Napoleonic wars, English Friends objected to the introduction of an income tax (largely for the war effort). In 1799, Quaker banker Nathaniel Morgan of Ross-on-Wye declared his unwillingness (on the grounds of conscience) to pay the new income tax devised by William Pitt the Younger to meet a spiralling war time deficit, and though it has never been formally accepted as a corporate witness by Yearly Meetings, to this day there are Friends who deduct the portion of income tax they believe will be allocated to military use.

The French and Indian War presented another challenge to John Woolman:

> orders came to the military officers in the county, directing them to draft the militia and prepare a number of men to go off as soldiers to the relief of the English at Fort William Henry in New York government.

A review which followed required drafting three times the originally expected number. As Burlington County was largely Quaker this created considerable consternation. But in his *Journal*, Woolman displayed appreciation facing the military:

> Amongst the officers are men of understanding, who have some regard to sincerity where they see it; and in the execution of their office, when they have men to deal with whom they believe to be upright-hearted men, to put them to trouble on account of scruples of conscience is a painful task and likely to be avoided as much as may be easily.

Woolman said that some of the young Quaker men went abroad until the conflict was over; some became soldiers and others 'appeared to have a real tender scruple in their minds against joining in wars and were much humbled under the apprehension of a trial so near.' With the latter he spent much time in counsel. In wars to come, this agonizing situation would be repeated by other young male American and British Quakers.

On 4th June 1758 orders came to Mount Holly to quarter about a hundred soldiers. Quartering in the colonies became a hot issue as only seven years later (1765) George Grenville (first Lord of the Treasury) put through a Quartering Act requiring the colonies to supply British troops with provisions and to provide them barracks. That on the heels of his loathsome Stamp Act fuelled revolutionary sentiments, and after independence was not forgotten, with the enactment of the 3rd Amendment to the Constitution which restricted quartering altogether. But in 1765, 'The cumulative effect of Grenville's measures raised colonial suspicion to a fever pitch.'[32]

31

Mount Holly, New Jersey.

32

When an officer came to John Woolman in 1758 asking that he, as with others in Mount Holly, provide 'lodging and entertainment for two soldiers' Woolman was told that he would be paid six shillings a week per man. As Woolman said, 'the case being new and unexpected, I made no answer suddenly,' but in the best of Quaker fashion he 'sat a time silent, my mind being inward.' Though, of course, convinced that war was 'inconsistent with the purity of the Christian religion,' Woolman said that he would not refuse the soldiers into his house, but also that he could not accept the payment. One of the company with the officer said that he thought Woolman might accept it as consistent with his religious principles. Characteristically, Woolman 'made no reply, as believing silence at that time best for me.'

In the end only one soldier was sent to Woolman's house and only for two weeks. Woolman said that the soldier 'behaved himself civilly.' At the end of the stay, Woolman went to the officer who lived nearby and told him 'on what grounds' he had refused the payment. One cannot help but wonder what – if any – effect Woolman's action had on the officer – or on the soldier he had entertained.

Out of Business and Travelling
in the Ministry

IN 1756 WITH THE Quakers deciding to withdraw from control of their province, John Woolman went out of business as well. He said that he 'grew uneasy on account of business growing too cumbersome.' He had started selling 'trimmings for garments ... clothes and linens' but other goods had followed. From his records we see just how much else:

> tea, thread, rum, molasses, butter, coffee, knitting needles, snuff, earthern dishes, chocolate, check, sheeting, tape, indigo, powder and shot, mettle buttons, silk, buckram, gloves and cedar board.

His trade 'increased every year and the road to large business appeared open; but I felt a stop in my mind.'

Most men would rejoice at such a development but not John Woolman. Like some other Quakers, Woolman was successful because he was trustworthy and customers knew they would not be overcharged or cheated. It was a two-edged sword for Quakers in business as James Walvin has recently explored:'(The) other-worldliness of Quakers had become ever more striking and increasingly difficult to defend, particularly when so many were achieving conspicuous commercial success ...'[33]

Woolman's 'business' was remarkably varied – and not just in goods sold. A single page from his account books indicates this:

	£	s.	d.
Samuel Hains's coffin and digging the grave	0	6	0
To Writing Indentures binding Gamaliel and			
Aquila to Trades	0	2	6

	£	s.	d.
To tracing the lines of the large lot back of the town, also the lot Budd bought, and Bargaining	0	3	6
To Assisting in Traceing the Lines and fixing Corners to the two parallels land sold Jos. Burr, and going to S. Cripses Concerning quit claim	0	6	0
The Estate of *Negro Maria* is charged 'For Cash paid Zach. Rossel for the two Children's passage up ye Mountholly Stage	0	4	0
Digging ye Grave	0	5	0
To self and horse two days in ye above Affair	0	10	0
To my time one day going to Mother's when Henry Burr took Isabella	0	4	0

Woolman was 36 when he retreated from retail merchandising; henceforth he would rely solely on tailoring and orchard-tending as his gainful occupations. This was also the year he began to write his journal. As he said:

I had in a good degree learned to be content with a plain way of living. I had but a small family (just his daughter, of course) that on consideration I believed Truth did not require me to engage in much cumbrous affairs ... It has been my general practice to buy and sell things really useful. Things that served chiefly to please the vain mind in people I was not easy to trade in, seldom did it, and whenever I did I found it weakens me as a Christian.

Many customers would miss his honesty, and again characteristically Woolman prepared them for his 'lessening of outward business.' He told them of his intentions and even suggested alternative shops they could use! But John Woolman was always doing that type of thing. Noting how often the poor got into debt he gave advice 'to take such goods as were most useful and not costly.' The custom of his day was to sell on credit and creditors often had to sue for non-payment. Once a constable gave Woolman a list of proceedings he had for a single year; he had served '267 warrants, 103 sumonses and 79 executions.' But only once did Woolman resort to the law to recover money when he 'had a warrant for an idle man who I believed was about to run away.'

With the fourth chapter of the *Journal*, Woolman recorded events as they occurred: from 1757 until his leaving for England. The fourth chapter begins with another of his dreams, this one as Olmsted writes, was one of those 'which are much less ordinary'.[34] In other words, it appears to be a vision, an experience when one is semi-conscious rather than wholly asleep.

Woolman had spent the night with Friends in Burlington 'and going to bed about the time usual with me. I woke in the night and my meditations as I lay were on the goodness and mercy of the Lord.' He went back to sleep but woke up again in the middle of the night. In what transpired Woolman was careful to say this was not a dream:

> It was yet dark and no appearance of day nor moonshine, and as I opened my eyes I saw a light in my chamber at the apparent distance of five feet, about nine inches in diameter, of a clear, easy brightness and near the center the most radiant. As I lay still without any surprise looking upon it, words were spoken to my inward ear which filled my whole inward man. They were not the effect of thought nor any conclusion in relation to the appearance, but as the language of the Holy One spoken in my mind. The words were, 'Certain Evidence of Divine Truth,' and were again repeated exactly in the same manner, whereupon the light disappeared.

Light, the Inner Light, the principle of Christian certitude, of course, is a cardinal Quaker notion and Woolman's 'words spoken to my inward ear which filled my inward man' well expressed the idea. Joshua Evans, a contemporary of Woolman about whom we will shortly hear, experienced a similar vision when 'bringing up my father's flock I saw the glory of the Lord shine round me which seemed to exceed the sun at noon-day.'[35]

Woolman's second trip south occurred in 1757; this time with his younger brother, Uriah, who at 27 moved to Philadelphia where he became successfully engaged in business. At 41, Uriah married

Susanna Burr whose father being the Surveyor-General of West Jersey was quite influential.

For Uriah the journey, not surprisingly, was a business trip and mainly to be in North Carolina. At first John appeared not comfortable having his brother as a companion. But after talking with several elderly Friends of Philadelphia, Uriah obtained 'a certificate suitable to the occasion' and they crossed the Susquehanna River over into Maryland. 'Soon after I entered this province,' John Woolman wrote, 'a deep and painful exercise came upon me.' It was, of course, because he knew these people 'lived on the labours of slaves.'

As Friends never charged for entertaining other members of the Society, Woolman's mind was troubled and then he came up with a solution. As the entertainment was made possible because of the slaves' labour, he left money to the family to be distributed to the Negroes. Needless to say, this made the Quaker heads of household rather uncomfortable – and that was just what Woolman hoped for. He said that he was surprised, however, 'that way was made easier than I expected, and few if any manifested any resentment at the offer, and most of them after some talk accepted of them.'

But in a subtle manner Woolman had pricked a few consciences and would continue to do so. On one occasion after breakfast, his host walked a way with him and Woolman had a conversation with him 'in the fear of the Lord concerning his slaves in which my heart was tender; and I used much plainness of speech with him, which he appeared to take kindly.'

Woolman's tender and plain speaking would slowly have an effect but also he began to encounter what now appear to be extremely odd justifications for slavery: 'Negroes were so wretched in their own country that many of them lived better here than there.' To that Woolman only said: 'There's great odds in regard to us on what principle we act.'

There was an even more absurd argument supposedly coming from Scripture. It is sometimes forgotten that up to the 19th-century with the appearance of the 'Higher Criticism', when it came to the Holy Bible, basically all Christians were literalists. The

Quakers were a bit different, believing that there was an even higher guide than the Bible – the Inner Light.

The argument from Scripture is rather convoluted: Ham the second son of Noah incurred a curse for his unfilial conduct. According to extra-biblical tradition, Ham was the forefather of the Ethiopians, Egyptians and Canaanites and his descendants were sentenced to be servants of servants – i.e. slaves. Frequently Bible believers presented the curse as justifying slavery, but Woolman appeared not to have taken it seriously and reminded one using the argument: '... the prophets repeatedly declared that the son shall not suffer for the iniquity of the father, but everyone be answerable for his own sins.' Woolman saw straight through such nonsense to the root cause of slavery – greed: 'The love and ease and gain are want to take hold of weak arguments to support a course which is unreasonable.'

During this second visit, Woolman toured the same Quaker settlements of lower Virginia and eastern Carolina where George Fox had been some seventy years earlier. The southernmost settlements he visited were in the Perquimans River area not far from Edenton. That section of North Carolina is particularly interesting because from there many long-established Quaker families later emigrated partly as a reaction against the slavery system which increased with the expanding production of tobacco. They went to the Northwest Territory (later Indiana) and that became a major Quaker centre (Richmond).

Before reaching the Perquimans River Woolman was at Cedar Creek near the James River staying with James Stanley. His son William had refused to bear arms for the side of the British in the French and Indian War, and that resulted in his imprisonment at Winchester. The staunchly Quaker Stanley family came from England in the early 18th-century settling in Hanover County, Virginia. William's imprisonment was two years before his marriage in 1758. The couple later moved to the Quaker settlement in Guilford County, North Carolina and were buried at New Garden.

As earlier noted, Woolman never ventured into the deep South but he must have been aware just how cruel and sinister slavery was developing in South Carolina and Georgia. But even what he experienced in Virginia and East Carolina distressed him. Little or no care was taken for slaves getting married and sometimes couples were parted with wives or husbands sold separately. Woolman also noted the use of the whip in the fields – a man was specially hired to do this. He also knew how little they had to eat: 'one peck of Indian corn and salt for one week' with some potatoes which they grew themselves 'on the first day of the week.'

Disobedience or slothfulness in work was severely punished and men and women 'have many times scarce clothes to hide their nakedness;' regularly boys and girls aged twelve were 'often stark naked amongst their master's children.' But despite this, Woolman noted that many Quakers taught the Negroes to read as did some of the New Light Presbyterians. In Virginia these sectarians had split from the parent body in 1741 during Whitefield's revivals.

Woolman's writings were beginning to have some positive effects. The Philadelphia Yearly Meeting in 1755 ordered that Friends who either imported slaves or purchased them in the area should be admonished. The Minutes of Burlington Monthly Meeting reported that it was 'clear of importing Negroes or purchasing them for life.' But this was only a small beginning.

Throughout their history Quakers have used what they call Advices and Queries to present guidance for the Society; these are regularly updated. As Philadelphia was the most influential meeting, its advices and queries carried weight elsewhere and consequently a committee of Virginia Yearly Meeting examined one of their queries in particular, one dealing with slavery: 'Are there any concerned in the importation of Negroes or buying them after imported?' The Virginia committee recommended to its members at their Yearly Meeting an altered version of the Philadelphia query which permitted buying slaves for one's own use if no further active participation in the slave trade were involved.

Woolman reached Virginia just as its Yearly Meeting at West Branch was occurring. There he tried to keep them from toning down the Philadelphia query. He said they 'appeared attentive to what was said; some expressed a care and concern for their Negroes; none made any objection by way of reply to what I said. But the query was admitted as they had altered it.' As Thomas

Drake has commented: 'Since even this decision was a step in advance, Woolman made no further protest.'[36] Unlike others Woolman recognized that any further action at that time might backfire.

However, Woolman noted progress elsewhere – in the Piedmont region of North Carolina, an area quite different from the plantation-developing area further east. A migration of Quakers from Pennsylvania and Virginia in the 1750s established New Garden in what became Guilford County. New Garden is now part of Greensboro and Guilford College, a Quaker institution, was founded there. New Garden became well known for the part it played in the Underground Railway, and appropriately it was in Greensboro in 1960 that the first Civil Rights sit-in demonstration occurred.

Woolman wrote an epistle on 29 May 1757 to the Friends Meeting at New Garden noting that he had been informed that

> there are a large number of Friends in your parts who have no slaves, and in tender and most affectionate love I now beseech you to keep clear from purchasing any ... Dwell here, my dear friends, and in remote and solitary deserts you may find true peace and satisfaction ...

The seed had been sown.

John Woolman displayed a remarkable tolerance toward other religious groups. William Penn's Holy Experiment had sealed a generous spirit in Pennsylvania and West Jersey when in the 1670s he made his religious tour of the Rhineland. Mennonites and like-minded Pietists were drawn to the Quaker colonies; soon outside Philadelphia they founded Germantown. Like the Quakers, the Mennonites were on the left wing of the Reformation. Their founder was the Anabaptist Menno Simons (hence their name) who stressed believers' baptism, a highly congregational church polity and opposed the taking of oaths, military service, as well as the holding of civic office.

Later the Amish came from the Mennonite movement, and today they are well known in Lancaster County for their opposition to automobiles, telephones and higher education. They wear plain clothing of a bygone era (hooks and eyes instead of buttons) and are remarkably efficient farmers. As the Quakers were also pacifists and for some time effected simple attire ('Quaker grey') in the public eye they were often confused with Mennonites and Amish.

Toward the end of chapter four and the record of his second journey south, Woolman gave the account of a member of the Mennonite society whom he called a 'Minoist'. Woolman said that at Menallen in Maryland 'a Friend gave me some account of a religious Society amongst the Dutch ...' Though founded in the Netherlands, most of the Mennonite immigrants were German and Pennsylvanians still live with the misnomer 'Pennsylvania Dutch' – i.e. Dutch for Deutsch. Woolman heard that a Mennonite planned to spend the night with an acquaintance 'of another society.' That was until he passed the acquaintance's fields and observed 'the distressed appearance of his slaves.' He had second thoughts and fixing a fire in the woods nearby spent the night there. Later the Mennonite's acquaintance heard what he had done and said that the Mennonite would have been 'heartily welcome' at his house.

The Mennonite responded:

Ever since I lodged by the field I've wanted to speak with thee. The matter was, I intended to come to thy house for entertainment, but seeing thy slaves at their work and observing the manner of their dress, I had no liking to come to partake with thee ... As I lay by the fire that night, I thought as I was a man of substance, thou would have received me freely, but if I had been as poor as one of thy slaves, and had no power to help myself, I should have received from thy hand no kinder usage than they.

Early in his *Journal* Woolman made some extraordinary remarks about religious affiliations. As a teenager he had said that he had 'found no narrowness respecting sects ...' Now in chapter five Woolman expanded that statement to 'All true Christians are of the same spirit but their gifts are diverse.' A remarkable irenical attitude at a time when polemics was the order of the day. He presented this statement in relationship to the writings of Thomas à

41

Kempis and added that 'in reading his writings I have believed him to be a man of a true Christian spirit.'

Thomas à Kempis (1380-1471) was a Dutch monk widely sought after as a spiritual adviser. He was also an ascetical writer and probably wrote *Imitation of Christ* which remains one of the most influential manuals of spiritual devotion of all time. Uniquely, the fact that the work was by a Catholic did not bother Woolman at all: '(Thomas à Kempis) laboured by a pious example as well as by preaching and writing to promote virtue and an inward spiritual religion.' Of course, Woolman must have been aware how contentious such an assessment would sound among Calvinists and Lutherans inhabiting New Jersey and Pennsylvania. In the same section as the foregoing, Woolman also mentioned the early Protestant martyr, John Huss who was burned at the stake in 1415, and spoke of how Huss 'contended against the errors (which) crept into the Church.' But characteristically, he coupled Thomas à Kempis with Huss and said that they were both 'of a true Christian spirit.'

The Catholic and the Protestant were 'sincere-hearted followers of Christ,' and this was during an age when many were still avidly consuming John Foxe's horrific 'Book of Martyrs' which vividly displayed religious persecutions. In his *Journal* Woolman referred to the book by its proper title *Acts and Monuments*. It was published in 1563 and became next to the Bible the most widely read book in the English language. It fuelled anti-Catholic sentiment for generations in Europe and America.

PART TWO

Like-minded Friends

SO FAR WE HAVE been following roughly the chronology given in Woolman's *Journal*, so now we come in chapter four to a section which Woolman devoted to John Churchman. It seems, therefore, an appropriate moment to discuss Churchman and other like-minded Friends who appear and re-appear in Woolman's writing.

Also this gives us an opportunity to discuss a larger issue of how closely linked Woolman was with those whom Jack Marietta called 'reformers'. Long before, Reginald Reynolds made the point that the journals of Joshua Evans and John Hunt

> often reflect the same spirit so that I have begun to wonder how far John Woolman's success was due to the fact that he was one of an ardent *group* of Friends, whose combined efforts were able to achieve far more than they could ever have effected without some unity between them, however informal the pattern of it may have been.[37]

Reynolds hoped that this omission would be picked up by a future historian.

In a sense Jack Marietta addressed himself to this omission, but whether Reynolds would have agreed with Marietta's presentation is another matter. In 1984, Marietta made his study of a 'Reformation of American Quakerism 1748-1783' largely based on over 10,000 disciplinary cases in the records of the Society of Friends. Not only does Marietta see a withdrawal of the Society from the forefront of Pennsylvania politics (largely due, of course, to the crisis of 1755) but also feels there developed a different vision from the one which inspired the Holy Experiment; nothing less than a reformation.[38]

Marietta's idea is not completely new: Frederick Tolles discussed the 'reformers' who sought to conserve the primitive Quaker values by purging away the compromises which had been made in

Pennsylvania.[39] There is no doubting that a change occurred in the Society (witness the large number of disowned offenders) but the idea that Churchman, Woolman, the Pembertons and others consciously set about reordering the Society stretches the point. What happened to the Society between 1748 and 1783 was not a 'reformation' as that word is usually employed in church history, and often Marietta's work appears to force material into bolstering a pet theory.

Be that as it may, in the first half of the 18th-century a number of Quakers shared common concerns and worked for the same goals of social and economic justice. We will now look at some of these men. The first, Benjamin Lay (1677-1759) was the most unusual and in his writing Woolman made no mention of him. Undoubtedly, however, he knew of Lay, and perhaps – at least – was unconsciously influenced by the 'histrionic zealot'. John Greenleaf Whittier referred to Lay and said that Benjamin Franklin knew him as well. *(See illustration of Benjamin Lay on page 141.)*

Apparently in 1738, Lay, who was a birthright Quaker, was disowned by the Society for 'some extravagance of conduct and language.' Lay had spent some years in the West Indies and there he became violently opposed to the practice of slavery. His behaviour so angered the planters that Lay was forced to leave the islands. After he settled in Philadelphia, Lay was shocked to find slaves there as well – and among Quakers. It is said that he fled city life and for a while, like a latter-day John the Baptist, lived in a cave, drinking only spring water and eating vegetables and refusing to wear 'any garment or eat any food purchased at the expense of animal life or which was in any degree the product of slave labour.'[40] Lay was only four and a half feet high, hunchbacked and covered his huge head with an enormous white hat. Whittier says that he was 'a figure to recall the old legends of troll, brownie, and kobold ... Such was the irrepressible prophet who troubled the Israel of slaveholding Quakerism ...'[41] And trouble them Lay did; not long did he stay in his cave. Soon he appeared frequently at Friends' meetings. The most spectacular occasion could have been in Woolman's presence as it occurred at Woolman's own monthly meeting in Burlington.

44

There in the midst of the usual silence Lay arrived in a long white overcoat. Dramatically stopping halfway in the meeting house he shouted: 'You slaveholders! Why don't you throw off your Quaker coats as I do mine, and show yourselves as you are?' Casting down the great white coat, the Friends assembled saw that Lay was wearing a military coat with a sword dangling at his trousers. 'In the sight of God' he continued, 'you are as guilty as if you stabbed your slaves to the hearts as I do this book.'[42] Lay's final histrionics was to stab the book he carried which contained a small bladder filled with the blood-coloured juice of poke-weed.

Catherine Owens Peare records another event and attributes its telling to Anthony Benezet:

(Lay) stole a neighbor's child and hid him all day. When the frantic parents finally came upon him and told him their story, he said, 'Your child is safe in my house, and you may now conceive of the sorrow you inflicted upon the parents of the Negro girl you hold in slavery, for she was torn from them by avarice.'[43]

Woolman could easily have known this event as well, but though he came to share Lay's loathing of slavery, his approach was dramatically opposite to that of Benjamin Lay. Ultimately Lay was a sad figure whose methods destroyed the effectiveness of his witness. Whittier also related that once Lay met with three other 'witnesses to the Truth' at Benjamin Franklin's house. They entertained an idea to 'convert all mankind to Christianity.' The three, however, got into such violent argumentation over theology that Franklin, a mildly interested listener, advised them to give up their project 'until they had learned to tolerate each other.'[44]

A Quaker quite unlike Lay and uncannily similar to John Woolman was Joshua Evans (1731-1798). Eleven years younger, Evans was a member of Mount Holly Particular Meeting and also wrote a journal. Both men had a distinct peace testimony and refused the use of any articles providing funds for military purposes. As with Woolman he would not use slave-grown products, and as will be discussed more fully, both men wore clothes of undyed cloth. The two were to suffer from their 'singularities', but Evans carried it further: he wore a beard at a time when that was

45

considered scandalous. Evans said that shaving was a human contrivance 'authorized through pride'.

In 1786, John Hunt gave an account of Evans' famous beard:

Met a committee appointed by our last select meeting held at Salem, on account of Joshua Evans' wearing his beard, and other singularities. The conference was long, but good order and good temper were maintained, tho' very different sentiments prevailed. It was a good edifying season, and I believe the opportunity will be useful; though he was left with his beard on, much as we found him, none having the power, or a razor to cut it off.[45]

The beard was not the only point to distinguish Evans' singularities from those of Woolman. Evans abstained from all animal products including leather. But the two were equally concerned about the welfare of Indians as well as Negroes. Evans survived Woolman by twenty-six years, and during the last year of his life (1798) was distressed by 'a party spirit that doth prevail throughout the land.'[46] This was at the time of the Alien and Sedition Acts, measures passed by Congress during a period of patriotic war fever which limited freedom of speech and the press and the liberty of aliens. These measures were largely aimed at Irish and French immigrants arriving in America.

Evans found the partisan spirit had

a strong tendency to break the unity, not only in kingdom and nation, but in neighbourhoods and families, and even amongst us as a people ... and to the lessening of the dignity of the high profession we make of promoting peace on earth ...[47]

Evans gave those words at a Quarterly Meeting of Friends and they were among his last.

John Hunt (1740-1824) will always be remembered by Quakers for the simple yet eloquent affirmation he made of their faith: 'Perfection does not consist in teaching truth, but in doing it.'[48] His father and John Woolman were first cousins: Elizabeth Hunt was the sister of John Woolman's father, Samuel. John Hunt was recorded as a minister and spent his life as a member of Chesterfield

Meeting in New Jersey. He was also a neighbour of Joshua Evans. Both Hunt and Evans were involved in giving aid to the Indians of Edgepellick and Brotherton and often visited among them.

Hunt is also known today for his interesting diary which gives insight into how Quakers suffered for their stand on slavery. 1798 was also recalled by Hunt but for a different tragedy: 134 Negroes who had been freed by North Carolina Quakers in the Albemarle Sound area (at considerable financial loss) were trapped by slave traders and sold back into slavery. This action hastened the Quaker migration to Indiana where several families took their Negroes with them to ensure their freedom. One of those families was celebrated in the popular book and film *Friendly Persuasion*.

Some ten years after John Woolman's death, John Hunt wrote:

Slavery now begins to be generally abhorred. Even the public newspapers manifest a dislike to the practice. A query in one of them says, 'and why is this cruelty practised? – Why, that we may have sugar to sweeten our tea, that debilitates us, and rum to put in our punch, which intoxicates us, and indigo to dye our clothes.' In short, great part of the human species are dragged into slavery to supply the luxuries of the rest.[49]

Like John Woolman, Anthony Benezet (1713-1784) deserves better appreciation in modern-day America, especially among the descendants of those whom he championed during his 71 years.

Benezet was born seven years before John Woolman, and for a Quaker, from a most exotic background. As George Brookes, his biographer says:

For seven hundred years the name Benezet has been revered in France. Call the roll of that family, and records will reveal saint and scholar, prophet and pedagogue, martyr and missionary who have benefitted mankind by their long and benignant service.[50]

The original seat of the family was in Languedoc, and Brookes begins with Saint Benezet (1165-1184) who promoted good roads, built the famous bridge at Avignon, and became the patron saint of engineers.

Centuries later, many Benezets became Huguenot and their attachment to Protestantism sealed the family's fate – especially when Louis XIV revoked the protective Edict of Nantes in 1685. Anthony Benezet was born in St Quentin and when he was two years old his parents took him to Holland. The journey of 170 miles was perilous but they made it in twelve days. However, as with the Pilgrims a hundred years earlier, the Benezets did not stay long in Holland and in 1715 arrived in England. Apparently young Anthony was placed in a counting house but being of a spiritual nature, like Woolman, he did not take to commercial interests. It is said he became a Quaker when he was only fourteen years old.

In 1731, the family (now seven children) moved to Philadelphia. Anthony's father had also attached himself to Quakerism but once settled in America, he became a member of the Moravian Church – already in England he had expressed interest in them.

In 1736, Anthony Benezet married Joyce Marriott, and for a time he tried manufacturing, but his heart was elsewhere and teaching became his lifetime passion. Benezet taught at Friends' schools in Germantown and Philadelphia and then he established an exemplary girls' school.

Frail health always plagued Benezet and twice he was forced to retire from teaching, but in both cases he returned. During one respite he found solace a bit like John Woolman with his fruit trees. However, Benezet discovered geese and once wrote: 'I often find more pleasure and instruction from the animal creation than the human.'[51] Benezet shared Woolman's love for animals and once when teaching some of his pupils decided to test their master's patience. Two boys placed a tiny mouse in a pillory on his desk. It didn't take long for Benezet to figure out which youths had done this, but instead of castigating them he released the mouse saying that at least they had mercifully imprisoned it instead of killing it. Apparently the action had a long and lasting effect upon the culprits.

As with Woolman and Benjamin Lay, Benezet's appearance was a matter of notice. In Benezet's case, it was what nature had sadly provided. One observer said Benezet was 'an old Quaker with a diminutive figure and humble and scanty physiognomy.'[52] Another was even more blunt: 'small and ugly, but his countenance wears the stamp of a peaceful soul, and the repose of a good conscience.'[53] Benezet never allowed himself to be portrayed and when a friend expressed a desire to have a portrait he responded: 'Oh, no, my ugly face shall not go down to posterity.'[54]

But perhaps it did in a round-about way. The frontispiece to Amelia Gummere's volume presented an alleged portrait of John Woolman. Janet Whitney, however, gave a convincing argument for it not being Woolman: so strongly she asserted: 'the evidence ... will not stand the test of even a slight examination.'[55] Henry Cadbury appears to agree: 'no where do we have a trustworthy portrait of (Woolman).'[56] Far more likely the alleged portrait was of Benezet: the most compelling evidence is that the original background was of a medal of the British and Foreign Anti-Slavery Association of which Benezet himself had supervised the execution.

However, it is appropriate that the two Quakers were often confused as their souls were intwined by common concerns and similar spirit. For twenty years they were intimate friends and in a letter of 1773, Benezet said to an associate that one of the greatest disappointments in life was not having more friends of 'John Woolman's spirit'. Benezet rarely spoke of Woolman in his letters except concerning their common associations but their nature was never to put on paper feelings for those close to them.

Anthony Benezet. Reduced from Amelia Gummere's frontispiece described above.

We do have another image of Benezet: this one is highly stylized and in *Historical Poetical and Pictorial American Scenes*. It was used as a frontispiece in Brookes' biography and shows Benezet instructing two coloured boys. That was Benezet's greatest moment: he was 'the first noted school teacher of poor Negro children in

America'[57] and devoted the last two years of his life to them. Upon his death his small fortune went to the school he founded for black children in 1770.

In 1802 Benjamin Rush (Philadelphia physician, politician and signer of the Declaration of Independence) wrote:

In one hand (Benezet) carried a subscription paper and a Petition; in the other he carried a small pamphlet on the unlawfulness of the Slave-Trade and a letter directed to the King of Prussia upon the unlawfulness of war.[58]

Unlike Woolman, Benezet was not shy to approach the lofty of his day and carried his concerns to the highest levels of politics and society. He wrote to men like Patrick Henry and John Jay, and the Reverend John Wesley. Benezet's *Some Historical Account of Guinea* (1772) so affected Wesley that he, as George Brookes says, 'In a century of free plagiarism presented an almost word for word duplication of Benezet as the opening chapter of his *Thoughts on Slavery.*'[59]

Both Benezet and Woolman were active in bettering relations with the Indians as well as the abolition of the slave trade. Benezet had begun his crusade against slavery in 1750 and with Woolman he joined other Quakers in sending the *Epistle of Tender Love and Caution* in 1755. But unlike Woolman, Benezet could be caustic and after hearing that George Whitefield had slaves at the orphanage in Savannah he wrote a strong letter to the Countess of Huntingdon (Whitefield's patron; he was her chaplain).

Benezet wrote to everyone it seems; there are 265 pages of his correspondence in Brookes' volume. In a letter of 1774 to John Wesley, Benezet quoted a grizzly advertisement from a North Carolina newspaper concerning a run-away slave. By this time, Methodism had taken firm root in the Carolinas. The advertisement read: 'Runaway Prince George ... a lusty Negro ... the said fellow is outlawed and I will give ten pounds reward for his head severed from his body, and forty shillings if brought home alive.'[60]

One interest of Benezet not to capture Woolman's attention was the plight of the French inhabitants in what came to be Nova Scotia. They were the Acadians and like many Indians, victims of the French and Indian War. The British considered the Acadians to be a threat to their position and forcibly resettled them in other British colonies to the south; most notably Louisiana where they became the Cajuns.

Despite the fact that the Acadians were Catholics and his family suffered persecution under French Catholicism, Benezet championed their cause and begged from door to door in Philadelphia for funds to shelter those Acadians who arrived in Pennsylvania. They could not have arrived at a worse time: July 1755 when General Braddock was defeated and the Delaware Indians (then wholly on the side of the French) were set loose on the frontiers of Pennsylvania. Not a time for anyone French to appear but that did not deter Benezet who also attempted to resurrect the former good relations with the Indians.

Benezet drew no distinction between helping Indians and French, Catholics and Protestants, Blacks and Whites. His writings had a great effect and he was also responsible for disseminating Woolman's works as well. Benjamin Rush said of Benezet: 'Few men, since the days of the apostles ever lived a more disinterested life.'[61] But the finest tribute of all came at his funeral in 1784: among the several hundreds who gathered at 'the largest funeral that had ever been seen in Philadelphia' (according to one observer) one third of the mourners were Blacks.

Rufus Jones once observed that over the years Quakerism produced two varieties of individuals; nowhere could the two be better viewed than in the Quaker colonies of Pennsylvania and New Jersey. The first group – smallish always – was totally committed to the Quaker ideal and 'If obedience to the soul's vision involves eye or hand, houses or life, they must be immediately surrended.'[62] Here were found men like Woolman, Hunt, Evans, Benezet and in his peculiar manner, Benjamin Lay.

The other group – a larger number – 'held it to be equally imperative to work out their principles of life in the complex affairs of the community and the state.'[63] That, of course, meant compromise and a certain submission to existing situations. Notable among the latter group, who were intimates of Woolman, was Israel Pemberton, Jr (1715-1779) known affectionately and derisively as

51

'the King of the Quakers'. The two leading Philadelphia Quakers of the second quarter of the 18th-century were Pemberton and James Logan. Of the two, Logan, a chief justice and successful fur merchant, was far more compromising.

Often overlooked in Quaker histories is just how significant the Quaker 'gentry' in Philadelphia became. Frederick Tolles reminds us:

> On the basis of fortune accumulated in overseas trade the Quaker merchants reared a structure of aristocratic living comparable to that of the Virginia planters, the landed gentry of the Hudson Valley, and the Puritan merchant princes of Boston.[64]

The notion of a Quaker aristocracy was, of course, a contradiction, and men like Israel Pemberton were extremely wealthy: the great trader's ships 'were seen in most of the major Atlantic ports.'[65] After two years governing the Pennsylvania province as President of the Council, James Logan escaped the pressures on his conscience and retired to his country estate. Israel Pemberton, however, remained in the thick of it, often acknowledging John Woolman's ideals. In a letter dated 7 June 1749, he even commended them to his brother, John:

> thou art at present disengag'd from incumbrances of many kinds, which is safer to avoid entering into, but hard to quit afterwards; thou knows how long I have been aiming at it, and having Labour'd under the difficulty am heartily desirous thou may be preser'd of Life and a Disposition of Mind to render thee ready and capable of improving the Gifts and Talents given thee to thy own eternal advantage ... Thou art sensible that by the Blessing of Providence a very moderate Care and industry will be sufficient, little more being necessary than to Keep from wasting what is already provided for us.[66]

Tolles says:

> John Woolman might almost have had Israel Pemberton in mind when he wrote with sympathy of those rich men who 'have at times been affected with a sense of their difficulties, and appeared desirous ... to be helped out of them, yet, for want of abiding under the humbling power of Truth, continued to be entangled in outward cumber.'[67]

Israel, Jr; James and John were the sons of Israel Pemberton, Sr (1684-1754) whose mansion, Evergreen, was on an estate of seventy-six acres. Israel, Jr had a hot temper on occasion and was often involved in argumentation in the Assembly: John Adams (to be the second American President) once called him 'that Quaker Jesuit.' Like other American revolutionaries, Adams loathed Quaker pacifism and noted how inconsistent it appeared with Pemberton's occasional fiery temperament. Brother James was another matter: quiet and a good influence on the family. John remained the diffident youngest brother. But all three brothers stood steadfastly by their pacifism and suffered because of it.

When the War of Independence came into full force, the Continental Congress advised the Council of the State of Pennsylvania to arrest and seize the papers of such citizens of Philadelphia as were 'notoriously British in their sympathies'. It also noted that 'a number of persons of considerable wealth who profess themselves to belong to the Society of people called Quakers ... are with much rancour and bitterness disaffected to the American cause.'[68] A list of 40 citizens was drawn up (many of them Friends) and included the three Pemberton brothers. They were arrested and imprisoned at Winchester, Virginia. Two other Quakers died while at Winchester and shortly afterwards so did Israel Pemberton. Never were British sympathies proven but in wars to follow pacifism continued to be a matter not easily understood or respected by the military.

The 'King of the Quakers' was a liberal patron of Philadelphia's institutions and was one of the founders of the Pennsylvania Hospital. It appears he advised Woolman on financial matters, and, with his two brothers, served on the original committee which edited Woolman's *Journal*.

After discussing the 1755 Yearly Meeting at Philadelphia, Woolman said that when he perused some notes his 'beloved friend' John Churchman made concerning 'our testimony against wars' he thought that he would place 'the substance of them' in his *Journal*.

John Churchman (1705-1775) was a life-long resident of Nottingham Township in Chester County. Although he was not Irish he grew up among Irish Quakers. Churchman was a farmer and a deputy surveyor of the province and started ministering at age 25. Reluctantly, a year later, he became an elder and to the dismay of those who promoted him, Churchman was seen as overly scrupulous in his duties and before long was replaced.

Churchman travelled a great deal: throughout America, Europe, Britain and Ireland, and he left a journal of those travels and his experiences. When he was 43 he was chosen a Justice of the Peace but declined the honour 'because God called him to avoid worldly cumbers.'

Jack Marietta says of his idea of the 'Quaker reformation' that it

> was not the work of any one person and no actor in it was irreplaceable. Yet it is possible to specify the first person to have expressed a hope to reform the Society and to have begun working at it. That was John Churchman.[69]

Churchman shared many of Woolman's views especially on the war tax and slavery, but his writing suffers in comparison to Woolman's. Janet Whitney observes: 'There is some evidence that Churchman was a little jealous of Woolman. His way of telling things in his journal sometimes seems to steal John Woolman's thunder.'[70]

In 1761 Woolman finished the second part of his *Considerations on Keeping Negroes* and submitted it for criticism to Churchman, Israel Pemberton and Anthony Benezet. There is evidence that at first the essay received a cold opinion from Churchman; not so with Pemberton and Benezet. The latter two recognized that Woolman was gifted but that his writing style could be very clumsy and over-extended. They were able to help with this, but it appears that Churchman could not easily get over a feeling that a younger light was outshining him.

However, the two men worked closely together, and as Churchman wrote:

> In this year (1759) I was engaged with my Friend, John Woolman, in visiting some active members of our Society who

kept slaves, first in the City of Philadelphia and in other places; also in New Jersey where we were enabled to go through some heavy labours and were favoured with peace.

This visiting was repeated two other times.

On his deathbed Churchman was reported to have said: 'I feel that which lies beyond death and the grave, which is now an inexpressible comfort to me.' Those present also remarked that 'Divine refreshment seemed to pour through him as a flowing stream,' and he uttered at the last: 'I may tell you of it, but you cannot feel it as I do.'[71]

Reginald Reynolds concludes his study of John Woolman in part by saying: 'I like to think of him now in the good company of men like Joshua Evans, Anthony Benezet and John Hunt, teaching a social gospel that did not divide.'[72] Reynolds' words remain the best last words on the relationship of Woolman to his like-minded Friends.

A
Firſt Book for Children.

Much uſeful reading being ſullied and torn, by Children in Schools before they can read, this Book is intended to ſave unneceſſary expence.

By JOHN WOOLMAN.

The third Edition enlarged.

ABCDEFGHIJKLMN
OPQRSTVUWXYZ

a b c d e f g h i j k l m n
o p q r ſ s t v u w x y z

Note. When the above Alphabet is defaced, this Leaf may be paſted upon the Cover, and the Alphabet on the other Side made uſe of.

PHILADELPHIA.
Printed, and Sold by JOSEPH CRUKSHANK, in Second-ſtreet; and by BENJAMIN FERRIS, Stationer and Bookbinder, in Wilmington.

See page 60.

Courtesy The Library Friends House, London.

PART THREE

'The Birth of Social Conscience in its Present-day Form'

FOR THE NON-QUAKER, certain nomenclature of the Society of Friends is baffling: Preparative Meeting, Monthly Meeting, Quarterly Meeting, Yearly Meeting. Actually it is fairly simple. The meeting I regularly attend is Richmond in Surrey – a Preparative Meeting, so-called because it prepares business for the Monthly Meeting which is the primary business meeting of the Society. It is Monthly Meeting which decides membership matters, so one becomes a member of a Monthly Meeting. In my case this is Kingston and Wandsworth MM. In John Woolman's day Monthly Meetings were further grouped into larger units, Quarterly Meetings which as the name suggests met quarterly in the year. That grouping has been largely replaced by regional General Meetings today which meet up to three times a year. Kingston and Wandsworth MM is a part of London and Middlesex General Meeting.

Yearly Meeting is the largest grouping of Quakers in most areas and as an annual gathering has important decision-making sessions. In Britain it used to be called London Yearly Meeting; now it is simply Britain Yearly Meeting. In John Woolman's case Mount Holly and Burlington Meetings were part of Burlington Quarterly Meeting which was part of Philadelphia Yearly Meeting.

In the summer of 1758 the Monthly Meeting of Philadelphia was concerned with the fact that some Friends had bought Negro slaves and moved that their Quarterly Meeting have a minute on the subject reconsidered in Yearly Meeting which had discussed the matter before. The point was whether Friends – as an organization – would speak out on the subject. John Woolman prepared himself.

As noted in the introduction, Dean Sperry dated 'the birth of social conscience in its present-day form' to 26th August 1758.

56

Woolman tells us that Philadelphia Yearly Meeting was to consider 'several weighty matters,' but the one in which he was interested came toward the end of deliberations. He was 'covered with inward prayer' and like David in the Bible 'tears were (his) meat day and night.' Woolman refrained from speaking on any other matter: 'the case of slavekeeping lay heavy upon me.'

But when he spoke it was brilliant and what needed to be heard. No one at the meeting tried to justify slavekeeping but – as always – there were those who were fearful that certain measures by the Yearly Meeting might 'give uneasiness to many brethren.' It was a time to be bold. John Woolman presented his case:

> My mind is often led to consider the purity of the Divine Being, and the justice of his judgments ... Many slaves on this continent are oppressed, and their cries have reached the ears of the Most High. Such are the purity and certainty of his judgments, that He cannot be partial in our favour. In infinite Love and goodness He hath opened our understanding from one time to another, concerning our duty toward this people; and it is not a time for delay. (my underlining) Should we now be sensible of what He requires of us, and through a respect to the private interests of some persons, or through a regard to some friendships which do not stand on an immutable foundation, neglect to do our duty in firmness and constancy, still waiting for some extraordinary means to bring about their deliverance, it may be that by terrible things in righteousness God may answer us in this matter.

When these words sunk in, Woolman observed:

> the love of the Truth in a good degree prevailed. Several Friends who had Negroes expressed their desire that a rule might be made to deal with such Friends as offenders who bought slaves in the future.

And so the door for freeing slaves owned by Quakers was opened wider. A thorough search would be made as to why Friends continued to keep Negroes, and those Friends would be visited. That would involve John Woolman.

It was the beginning of the end. Philadelphia Yearly Meeting decided to exclude slave buyers from positions of authority in the business affairs of the Meeting, and twelve years after Woolman's death, Yearly Meeting made disownment the penalty for selling or transferring slaves. In doing this, the Quakers became the first large group in America to free their slaves. And Tolles says of Woolman's role:

> More than any other single influence, it was Woolman's clear and steady voice that woke the conscience of the Quakers and ultimately, through them, of the Western world to the moral evil of slavery.[73]

Unlike Benjamin Lay, John Woolman was no solitary prophet: rather he was totally committed to the structure, discipline and support of the Quaker community. Reading through meeting minutes which survive, it soon becomes apparent just how involved he was in the corporate Quaker witness.

Woolman's life as a Quaker spokesman began at age 22 when he was first recorded a minister of Burlington Monthly Meeting. For seventeen years he was Clerk of meeting, a representative to Philadelphia Yearly Meeting, and for sixteen years he was a member of the Overseers of the Press for Yearly Meeting as well.

This aspect of Woolman cannot be overestimated as it was why members of the Society came to know and trust him, and it is also why they came to listen to him as well. He faithfully attended meetings for business – and what an experience that is as all new Quakers come to know. Quaker meetings for business are quite unique and usually occur after meetings for worship, and as with worship they aim to discover the will of God. Quakers do not vote and there is neither majority nor minority rule. The Clerk of meeting is given the unenviable task of 'discerning the sense of the meeting', and that usually takes time. If no sense of the meeting can be discerned, no decision is taken and no minute recorded other than that the meeting was not ready to proceed. Those accustomed to quick and dictatorial decision-making find this procedure frustrating indeed.

When I first became Clerk of my Preparative Meeting I recalled some comments Woolman made in the sixth chapter of his *Journal*. He discussed Quarterly Meetings as being 'large' and sitting for 'near eight hours'. Mercifully that is unheard of these days, but

Woolman's words which followed this observation remain appropriate to Clerks and those attending meeting for business:

> First, except our minds are rightly prepared and we clearly understand the case we speak to, instead of forwarding, we hinder business and make more labour for those on whom the burden of the work is laid.
>
> If selfish views or a partial spirit have any room in our minds, we are unfit for the Lord's work. If we have a clear prospect of the business and proper weight on our minds to speak, it behooves us to avoid useless apologies and repetitions. Where people are gathered from far, and adjourning a meeting of business attended with great difficulty, it behooves all to be cautious how they detain a meeting, especially when they have sat six or seven hours and a good way to ride home.

With all his other activities it is hard to believe that from time to time John Woolman was also a schoolmaster. Unlike his friend, Benezet, however, his teaching was not salaried and was intermittent. The two did often confer on teaching methods and interests and that came to involve a remarkable young lady, Rebecca Jones, whose school Woolman emulated in Mount Holly.

Rebecca was the daughter of two pious Anglican parents but it appears that her father, a seaman, was lost at sea when she was quite young. Rebecca became a Quaker when she was fifteen, and when her mother died in 1761 she took her place as head of a girls' school. Rebecca was only 22 but soon proved herself as very successful; she, Woolman and Benezet frequently discussed educational notions and experiences. Janet Whitney gives a clear impression that Woolman was fond of 'Becky'. On one particularly bitter winter Sunday Woolman was in Philadelphia visiting a cousin and not far from Becky's home. There had been a heavy snow and Becky gave up the possibility of attending Meeting. But when she heard a noise at the door she opened it to discover John Woolman,

> like a snowman, banging his shovel and stamping the snow off his feet. He suggested that she should invite him to breakfast – he thought he'd earned it ... he had dug her a path all the way to Bank Meeting-house in Front Street.[74]

Janet Whitney also suggests that Woolman's interest in education started with his daughter, Mary's 'earliest years'. Though his *Journal* made no mention of teaching, even a casual perusal of Monthly Meeting minutes and Woolman's account books indicates how much teaching Woolman did. His primer, *A First Book for Children* went through three editions. It is not known when this charming school book for teaching children how to read and write was first issued but Amelia Gummere thinks it may antedate both Benezet's own primer and Christopher Sauer's which he published in 1770 and has been called 'the earliest book in Pennsylvania on the subject of schoolteaching.'[75]

Woolman and Benezet often worked together on composing suitable mottoes for their pupils to copy, but many of Woolman's have no moral content. They are a refreshing change from the grim Puritan hornbooks designed to instill the fear of God. Often Woolman was satisfied to delight in nature: flowers, rain, and lambs. One example gives us the feeling:

> *The Dove doth no harm,*
> *The Lamb doth no harm,*
> *A good boy doth no harm.*
> *The eye of the Lord is on*
> *them that fear him. He*
> *will love them, and do*
> *them good.*
> *He will keep their Feet in*
> *the way they go, and save*
> *them from the Paths of*
> *Death.*[76]

In Woolman's larger account book there are records for teaching the children of his brothers Asher and Abner, and those of Aaron Burton, Thomas Bispham, James Dobbin, John Sleeper and others. We find charges for spelling books, writing materials, ink powder and such. But on the same page as these was also the cost of grafting trees, hickory wood for the meeting house, estimates for jackets and trousers. Woolman was busy.

In late 1758 Woolman joined Daniel Stanton, John Scarborough and John Sykes in visiting Friends who had slaves.

Scarborough was active in Philadelphia Yearly Meeting and was sixteen years older than Woolman. Sykes was even older and a frequent travelling companion. Daniel Stanton (1708-1770) once was called by Rebecca Jones 'that beloved Friend and Father in the Truth'. He was born in Philadelphia but his father was lost at sea before his birth and his mother died soon after. Stanton was brought up by a brother of his mother in New Jersey and was apprenticed to a ship's carpenter. Afterwards he learned the trade of a joiner. His family life continued to be tragic: his wife of fifteen years died suddenly and four of their sons before her death. Of his two daughters only one survived into Stanton's later years.

Stanton travelled extensively: Barbados, Antigua and Ireland. He also served with Woolman on the Yearly Meeting's committee to visit slaveholders near Philadelphia, and as we will see, Stanton was also involved with bettering relations with the Indians. He died two years before Woolman and at the house of Israel Pemberton.

Woolman spoke of the visits to Friends with slaves as 'edifying ... where the channel of gospel love was opened and my mind was comforted after a hard day's work,' but in the spring of 1759 after visiting 'some of the more active members ... who had slaves' he made an interesting admission:

Having at times perceived a shyness in some Friends of considerable note toward me, I found an engagement in gospel love to pay a visit to one of them, and as I dwelt under the exercise I felt a resignedness in my mind to go; so I went and told him in private I had a desire to have an opportunity with him alone, to which he readily agreed. And then in the fear of the Lord, things relating to that shyness were searched to the bottom, and we had a large conference which I believe was of use to both of us, and am thankful that way was opened for it.

This is a good example of what Michael Heller has termed John Woolman's 'soft persuasion.' Heller makes the important observation – often overlooked by other commentators – that it was 'Woolman's special genius that he would draw from his Quaker upbringing an understanding of how he might speak and write in a way that would deeply move both Quakers and non-Quakers.' His 'special genius' originated in the very customary approach of

Quaker worship. Because Quakers had done away with ritual and 'because language was given a secondary place within the larger context of silence, speaking in the Quaker meeting took on a renewed significance.'[77] When Friends spoke it was not like the Puritans or George Whitefield in the fiery oratory of the pulpit but out of the quiet of Meeting. Woolman carried that approach with him out of the Meeting House into the world. He was with the 'Friend of considerable note' alone, quiet, face to face.

Secondly, Woolman never attacked the slaveholders directly; he never ranted as later abolitionists would. Woolman concentrated on what effects holding slaves had on the master and his children. It was a quiet, slow, soft friendly persuasion – and in time it had its fruits. It disarmed and spoke to the better nature. Never did he come down on the sinner as wicked, demanding immediate change as was the case in the emotionally-charged revivals sweeping the colonies. After all, conversion was a life-long process, not something sparked at a moment – and easily left in the next change of heart.

In the winter of 1759 an outbreak of smallpox occurred in Mount Holly. Woolman reported 'many' were 'inoculated of which a few died ...' There remains historical confusion concerning this the most devastating disease of the 17th and 18th centuries. This highly infectious virus with its permanent pitted scars ravaged the colonies and decimated Indian tribes. The Aztecs portrayed it as a plague from the Europeans (which was what it was) but it became a worldwide phenomenon. In the East because it was noted as seldom attacking the same person more than once, there was a deliberate inflicting of healthy people with a mild form of the disease in order to give them immunity from a more dangerous form.

This did not always work but the remarkable world traveller, Lady Wortley Montagu (1689-1762) introduced the practice into England and it was carried to the colonies. It was this inoculation to which Woolman referred. It was only in 1796 that Edward Jenner came up with a workable solution: he had observed that milk-maids never appeared to get smallpox. The reason was that they contracted a mild disease, cowpox, which did offer a satisfactory immunity. This discovery led to Jenner's vaccination we know so well today. It was so successful that in 1979 it was declared that smallpox was eradicated worldwide.

Woolman's attitude toward smallpox, therefore, must be understood in this context. He must have been aware that inoculation as practised in 1759 did not ensure immunity from the disease which had taken his beloved sister in 1747. However, it is difficult for us to accept the seeming fatalism of his remarks:

> The more fully our lives are conformable to the will of God, the better it is for us. I have looked at the smallpox as a messenger sent from the Almighty to be an assistant in the cause of virtue, and to incite us to consider whether we employ our time only in such things as are consistent, with perfect wisdom and goodness.

Having said that, Woolman also stressed the necessity of 'building houses suitable to dwell in ... preparing clothing suitable for the climate and season, and food convenient, are all duties incumbent on us.'

Woolman, however, was also uncomfortable with the extremes his neighbours took to avoid the disease: closing up their houses, fleeing Mount Holly, refusing to have visitors, taking frequent bleedings and burning vile sulphur. He further wondered whether some used the epidemic as an excuse for not continuing activities which benefited those in need:

> Do affairs relating to civil society call me near this infection? If I go, it is at the hazard of my health and life, and becomes me to think seriously whether love to truth and righteousness is the motive of my attending ...

This would not be the end of Woolman's wrestling with such questions – or his encountering the horrible smallpox.

With the lessening of the smallpox outbreak, Woolman made his second journey into New England in the spring of 1760. On his way he stopped in Long Island and from Jericho he wrote the only letter to his wife recorded in the *Journal*:

We are favoured with health, he said, and added: I have often found an engaging love and affection toward thee and my daughter and friends about home (so) that going out at this time, when sickness is so great amongst you, is a trial upon me ... I feel my mind resigned to leave you for a season, to exercise that gift which the Lord hath bestowed on me ...

This was an especially important visit as other Yearly Meetings in America had not yet gone as far as Philadelphia's stand. Newport was particularly significant for Woolman to visit: from there Quaker ships loaded down with rum were involved in the insidious triangular trade to Africa and back to slave markets in the New World.

Recently Hugh Thomas emphasized the importance of Newport: 'Rhode Island carried just over 150,000 slaves from Africa to the Caribbean or to North America, probably 100,000 were financed by merchants of Newport.'[78] The Quaker involvement sickened Woolman:

The great number of slaves in these parts and the continuance of trade from there to Guinea made deep impression on me, and my cries were often put up to my Father in secret, that he would enable me to discharge my duty faithfully in such ways as He might be pleased to point out to me.[79]

The powerful Quaker Redwood family owned slave plantations and Thomas Richardson, clerk of the New England Yearly Meeting participated in the slave trade. Abraham Redwood was

among the first North Americans to carry commercial logic to its geographical conclusion by not only trading in Newport and Africa but a plantation in Jamaica, to which his own ships took slaves from Africa.[80]

Woolman met some support in New England Yearly Meeting, but as Thomas Drake relates:

his arguments failed to convince the weightier and wealthier Friends of slave-trading Newport. One of them even left a session of the Yearly Meeting while Woolman was there for the purpose of selling some slaves which had just arrived on one of his ships.[81]

When Woolman heard this his 'belly trembled' and his 'lips quivered.' His appetite also failed and he 'grew outwardly weak.'[82]

But the episode also fired Woolman to draw up a petition to the Rhode Island Assembly which was in session. He planned to present his case as they sat in Newport: 'I was desirous that Friends might petition the Legislature ... for I saw this trade was a great evil ...' Unfortunately the Assembly adjourned before Woolman could attend, so he next turned his attention on 'leading active members about Newport being in the practice of slavekeeping.' Apparently Woolman's meeting with them had a good effect and he could say: 'I took leave of them in a good degree of satisfaction ... several of them expressed in relation to disposing of them (slaves) after their decease.'

Slower than Philadelphia, in 1770 New England Yearly Meeting finally strengthened their query on slavery to discourage selling as well as buying slaves and not long after, slave trading ceased among New England Quakers. This was partly due to men like Thomas Hazard whom Woolman had met during his first visit north. Thomas's father, Robert, was the largest slave owner in Rhode Island with an estate of 12,000 acres (the average farm of the day was 200-300 acres). In 1742, the tall and handsome Thomas had married a Quaker and to his father's horror lived simply (and freed the slaves) on the well-stocked farm his father had given the couple as a wedding gift. As Thomas Drake tells us: 'he had more reason for using slaves on his rich South County farm than had Friends anywhere else in New England.'[83] Woolman's friendship had come at just the right time and Hazard laboured the rest of his life for the abolition of slavery. Fourteen years after Woolman's second visit (1774), an act was passed in the Assembly which prohibited the importation of slaves as well as stating that all slaves entering Rhode Island from the outside world would automatically be free men. Thomas Hazard was one of the leaders for this reform.

Just before leaving Newport for Nantucket (17 June 1760) Woolman wrote his brother Abner:

Dear Brother,

I have remembered (since I left home) thee and thy family very often with much nearness of love.

We are at Newport and expect to go for Nantucket soon, if way open. We have been fellow feelers with the afflicted, nor is any affliction too great to endure for the Truth. This I own, and am labouring daily to be found in that resignation.

I am pinched for time, but wanted to let thee know I often think of you.[84]

Six days later Woolman wrote his wife that he 'was not so hearty and healthy as I have been'. He rarely complained about his health but from various accounts we know that he laboured throughout his life under a fairly frail exterior. Reaching Nantucket was about two days sail, but he was pleased with the simple life he found among the hearty island Friends: quite a contrast from Newport. On this visit Woolman noted the hazardous environment so dependent on the weather and the mainland for goods. He also observed that the whales 'being much hunted and sometimes wounded and not killed, grew more shy and difficult to come at.'

Twenty-one years later John Churchman's son, George, visited Nantucket and also noted there a great contrast to Philadelphia Quakerism. Farms and pastures were pooled 'in a kind of joint Commonwealth ... Social, friendly & commendable way of living.'[85] But already the seeds of destruction were being sown. As Woolman noted the whales had been over-hunted and in the next century the profitable industry collapsed. And so did Nantucket Quakerism. Disownment of members for trivial offences turned the Friends into a stifling moralizing group set apart on their island and ironically not so different from the Puritan society from which the first settlers had escaped.

'Some Instruction from Them'

WE DO NOT KNOW exactly when John Woolman started wearing undyed clothing, but it appears to be not long after his return from his second visit to New England. Some writers have given the impression that Woolman wore undyed clothing all his adult life; the truth is that it was only for the last decade. Like Benjamin Lay it was part of a larger protest against goods provided through slave labour: sugar, molasses, rum and silverware. South American silver was mined by slaves in appalling conditions and dyes (such as indigo) came from slave labour in the West Indies as did sugar. Woolman did not begin all at once to discard 'hurtful dyes': so called because they masked dirt and contaminants. He said: 'I felt easy to wear my garments heretofore made, and so continued about nine months.'

Then he purchased a hat the natural colour of the fur. This 'singularity' made Woolman feel uneasy as 'natural' fur hats were becoming the latest fashion: 'some Friends were apprehensive that by wearing such a hat savored of an affected singularity.' To us it appears a humorous twist but, as we will see, Woolman and his friends would find the increasingly 'all-white' attire made the Quaker minister an object of considerable attention.

The years 1761 to 1763 were a busy period. Woolman finished his journey to New England in August 1760, and it appears that the following winter he wrote the second part of his *Considerations on the Keeping of Negroes* which was published at his own expense by Benjamin Franklin in 1762. After some further visitations to slaveholders in and around Philadelphia and central New Jersey, Woolman made his extraordinary visit to Indians some 200 miles up the Susquehanna River.

Alistair Cooke once said:

When it was plain that the white man had come to stay, there were three things he could do with the natives. He could, as William Penn did, treat them as separate nations to respect and live with. (This Christian approach would work with some tribes and not with others.) He could treat them as a potential threat, skirmish and parley and hope for a continuing truce. Or he could treat them as annoying primitive obstacles to the extension of civilization. This view, it is no secret, prevailed among all but the most enlightened pioneers.[86]

Well known is Benjamin West's painting of William Penn's treaty with the Indians under a great elm tree in 1682 at Shackamaxon, the Indian 'place of the kings' near the banks of the Delaware River. West painted the scene in 1764 and Penn and his associates are pictured in Quaker dress fifty years later than the event. West's Penn became popular and was the inspiration for the Quaker Oats man; for long in America this has been the popular image of the Quaker.

Penn was said to have arrived at Shackamaxon in the Governor's barge and spoke words something like these:

The Great Spirit who made me and you who rules the heavens and the earth, and knows that I and my friends have a hearty desire to live in peace and friendship with you, and to serve you to the utmost of our power. It is not our custom to use hostile weapons against our fellow creatures, for which reason we have come unarmed.[87]

Today it is doubted that Penn's agreements with the natives occurred in the manner West depicted: the Shackamaxon 'treaty' was more a symbol of decent treatment and involved many negotiations over a period of years. Penn and his associates were not the first to buy rights to lands from the Indians either: the Dutch and the Swedes who had come earlier did not settle on unpurchased soil. Contrary to popular opinion, Penn had no use to purchase large sections of land; only a little strip along the Delaware.

For the time, however, Penn's treatment of the Indians was extraordinary: 'He approached them as equals,'[88] and learned their customs. Willis Rivinus, an historian of the Delaware Indians, has said that Penn was 'a knowledgeable, sensitive and inquisitive observer ... His first person accounts are probably as revealing as any we are likely ever to find.'[89] Penn knew what he was talking about: he walked with the Indians, sat with them on the ground, and ate their roasted acorns and homony grits. He was one of the few to learn their difficult language. The developing relations were so good that no Quaker blood was ever shed by an Indian and there were no serious disturbances for seventy years – until 1756 when the government passed from Quaker hands at the French and Indian War.

One Indian chieftain was reported as saying of the 'Quakels' – as his tribe called them – that they could not be Christians as they neither got drunk nor quarrelled. Drink indeed was the demon for Indians who often could not control their use of alcohol and frequently they were given drink by settlers to take advantage of their intoxication. In that state false maps were given, faulty weights were used in measuring their furs – and worse of all – the natives had no recourse to justice. However, as Rufus Jones said: 'From these things the Pennsylvania Indians were preserved.'[90]

But by the time William Penn died in 1718, the situation had started to change. When the Europeans arrived, the Lenape (Delaware) Indians were among the most culturally advanced of all the North American tribes. They tried to meet the white man half-way but in the end they suffered the same fate as the more belligerent tribes to the north and west.

A number of factors changed matters greatly: the depletion of the beaver supply which was the major trading in the early days; the Indians' addiction to blankets, guns and rum. And the natives never understood the white man's concept of land ownership: for them man was a transitory visitor in relatively abundant surroundings. The gun – which only the settlers supplied – changed all the Indians' rules of hunting forever. As if all this were not enough, there were the new diseases brought into his environment. The mortality figures are horrendous: in the first one hundred years of contact (1550 to 1650) diseases like smallpox, measles and typhus wiped out between two-thirds to three-quarters of the entire Indian population along the Atlantic coast.

As often happens in history, the sons of William Penn did not share their father's spirit and vision: Willis Rivinus puts it more bluntly: 'Not one of his thirteen children took after their father, in ability or interest in the growth of his province.'[91] William Penn, Jr visited Pennsylvania in 1704, but after a few weeks was involved in a public brawl: he was a wild youth, a non-Quaker and a heavy drinker. Thomas Penn managed his father's interests from 1732 to 1741, but he too was another disappointment. Increasingly an absentee Proprietor, Thomas preferred London to Philadelphia, married the daughter of the Earl of Pomfret and embraced Anglicanism. In 1737 he violated the spirit of previous agreements with the Indians with the saga of the Walking Purchase.

It is a complicated affair which greatly shocked many Quakers; unfortunately recent historians of the North American Indians isolate the event from otherwise fair dealings in Pennsylvania. Desiring more lands, Thomas Penn produced a deed allegedly signed by his father and three Lenape chiefs in 1686 which ceded all their lands around the forks of the Delaware (west of the Neshaminy Creek) as far as a man could go in 'a day and a half.' William Penn used to do these walks with the Indians himself, but this deed had never been walked – and later was discovered to be a forgery. Alvin M. Josephy makes much of the event in a recent study:

Pennsylvania ... applied anything but honorable thinking to the settlement. Its leaders advertised for athletes, offering land incentives and money to whoever could go the longest distance in the allotted time. Agents were sent out to find the fleetest men, and three were finally selected. They were trained for nine days over the terrain they would walk, while workers slashed and cleared brush from the path they would follow.

What was called the Walking Purchase was consummated on August 25, 1737. When the walk began, crowds of spectators lined the path, cheering on the participants – who loped rather than walked. From the sidelines also, Lenapes called repeatedly to the athletes to walk, not run. Of the three athletes, only one lived through the ordeal, and he fell prostrate at the end of the day and a half. He had covered sixty-four miles, securing for the whites approximately twelve hundred square miles of the Indians' lands.[92]

As we have seen, matters got worse with the French and Indian War and the end of Quaker rule in 1754. John Fothergill, English physician and Quaker leader, wisely reminded his religious compatriots in Pennsylvania that 'your kingdom is not of this world.'[93] Like other Quakers he saw that their energies could more appropriately be turned into philanthropic pursuits.

But change was obvious for other reasons: by 1750, Quakers made up only 25% of Philadelphia's population and the Scotch-Irish Presbyterians (with their hardened attitudes toward the natives) were becoming the dominant force. With them, the gentry found the Church of England more to their liking especially in the light of its new able clerical leadership: two-thirds of the signers of the Declaration of Independence were Anglican. Quaker influence would have to find new directions.

In 1756 'The Friendly Association for gaining and preserving Peace with the Indians by pacific means' was founded by Israel Pemberton and like-minded Friends. It endeavoured to further trade with the Indians. A similar organization was set up in New Jersey under the leadership of Samuel Smith and the first Indian reservation ever in America was established at Brotherton in Burlington County. There New Jersey Indians were settled on 3,000 acres.

In the eyes of many non-Quakers these actions in the aftermath of the Indian attacks in western Pennsylvania added insult to injury. In December of that year Samuel Fothergill (John's brother) wrote from Philadelphia to his wife:

The consternation in which this province hath been thrown by the Indians is not diminished. The Assembly have sold their testimony as Friends to the people's fears, and not gone far enough to satisfy them; the Indians have complained without redress, and are now up in arms, and have destroyed many people; there were the bodies of two men whom the Indians had killed and scalped, brought down in great parade to this city, from the back parts; multitudes went to see them, and seem loudly to clamour for war. The ancient methods of dealing with the Indians upon the principles of equity and justice seem neglected, the spirit of war and destruction endeavouring to break loose, in order to reduce this pleasant, populous province to its ancient wilderness condition.[94]

The mangled bodies of the murdered settlers enraged Philadelphians and John Churchman wrote in his diary that many people not only cursed the Indians but 'also the Quakers'. But Israel Pemberton refused to lessen his efforts:

> The name of a Quaker of the same spirit as William Penn still is in the highest estimation among (the Indians') old men, and there is a considerable number of us here united in a resolution to endeavor by the like conduct to fix the same good impression of all of us in the mind of the rising generation.[95]

In this spirit two conferences were held at Easton in 1756 and 1758. At the first, the 'King of the Delawares' Teedyuscung, refused to appear unless Quakers were there. Again the Indians complained about land frauds and the Governor promised to redress the wrongs. But at the second conference the Lenape were further humiliated and told to move west. The same fate of all Indians awaited them.

Despite Quaker attempts to reinstate feelings presented earlier by Penn, the handwriting was on the wall. Probably for the Lenape, the ultimate indignity had occurred in 1756 when the Governor and his Council at the outset of the French and Indian War had declared the Lenape tribe to be 'enemies, rebels and traitors to his Most Sacred Majesty.' Thomas Penn – in an action which would have horrified his father – offered

> a bounty on Indian scalps for which subscriptions were raised in the Philadelphia coffee houses and taverns for the defence of the frontiers. The bounty was $130 for a male scalp and $50 for a female scalp. Although the bounty was intended only for the battlefield, its impact on the remaining 'friendly' Lenape was devastating. The Quaker members of the Assembly resigned in disgust.[96]

With the Peace of Paris ending the French and Indian War in 1763, Britain took all of France's North American possessions east of the Mississippi River. Between the thirteen colonies and the Louisiana territory was a large area designated as 'Indian Reserve': it would not remain so for very long.

From childhood John Woolman had well known the native Americans. A twenty-foot square schoolhouse down the Rancocas was where he and other white children were taught side by side with Indian youth. The little log Meeting House the Woolman family attended was built beside an old Indian burial ground where the early settlers also buried their dead. When Quakers went to Meeting often Indians looked after their young. In his *Journal* in 1762, Woolman said why he wanted to visit among the natives: 'Having many years felt love in my heart toward the natives of this land who dwell far back in the wilderness, whose ancestors were the owners and possessors of the land where we dwell ...'

In August 1761, while on a visit to some Philadelphia Quakers who held slaves, Woolman met some natives who lived on the east branch of the Susquehanna River at an Indian town called Wyalusing some 200 miles northwest of Philadelphia. The encounter crystallized Woolman's intention and so in the winter of 1762 he presented his plans to Monthly and Quarterly Meetings. It is noteworthy that as with his efforts on behalf of black slaves, Woolman never proceeded entirely on his own. He always worked within the framework of Quaker organization and discipline. But at this time 'To go was to take his life in his hands.'[97] The night in May 1763 he was to leave, with everyone asleep, some Philadelphia Quakers arrived at Mount Holly to warn Friend John. An express rider had just reached them in Philadelphia with word of an uprising at Pittsburgh to the west: some English had been scalped and slain.

Woolman listened to them and then returned to bed without waking his wife. The next morning when he told her the news 'she appeared to be deeply concerned ... but in a few hours my mind became settled in a belief that it was my duty to proceed ...' Long-suffering Sarah, how she must have wondered about her John at times. But off he went, first stopping briefly at the Monthly Meeting at Burlington and then accompanied by Israel and John Pemberton, he crossed the Delaware. Israel went to Philadelphia the next morning and the remaining two arrived at Samuel Foulke's place in Richland, Bucks County. There Benjamin Parvin, a 36-year-old Irish-born Quaker surveyor, determined to go with Woolman. At first Woolman was against this: he did not want to involve Parvin in the potential danger ahead, but 'Benjamin appeared to be so fastened to the visit that he could not be easy to leave me.' They joined William Lightfoot and the three arrived at Bethlehem.

Today Bethlehem is largely known for its great steel industry, but it was founded by a deeply religious sect, the Moravian Brethren in the 1740s. The Moravians had a curious history: originally they were survivors of the Hussite reform of the 15th century. They were 'renewed' at Herrnhurt under Count Nicholas von Zinzendorf in 1722. He was a Pietistic Lutheran who remoulded the Hussite brethren into a highly evangelistic sect with an obsession over the atonement of Christ. Their community at Bethlehem thrived and they were active in missionary work among the Indians. On his journey Woolman would encounter the greatest missionary among them, David Zeisberger. Once he settled in Pennsylvania, Zeisberger, a brilliant linguist (who easily acquired various Indian dialects) made numerous converts in the valleys of the Lehigh and Susquehanna rivers during sixty years among the Indians.

After Bethlehem and a short stop at Fort Allen, Woolman and Parvin were alone as Lightfoot went his own way. Soon they encountered an Indian trader recently arrived from Wyoming who told them how white settlers were getting Indians intoxicated so as to cheat them out of skins and furs they had acquired with great labour. On 10th June they crossed the Lehigh River, and now they were in the company of some Indians on their way to Wyalusing. An Indian who had killed a deer shared it with Woolman's company, and having pitched a tent, Woolman took note of some Indian drawings on the sides of large trees. He mused about these historical records 'painted mostly in red but some with black,' and thought of the 'innumerable afflictions' these 'proud, fierce' people endured: 'miseries and distresses when wounded far from home,' how they chased 'one another over the rocks and mountains.' And then he contemplated the hatred 'which mutually grows up in the minds of the children of those nations engaged in war.' With these 'meditations' – as he called them – was 'the desire to cherish the spirit of peace amongst these people arose very fresh in me.'

Woolman rarely complained of discomfort but we read that he and his companions were already wet when they came to lodge in the woods; the ground and the tent was damp as well as the bushes

74

surrounding them. The next morning he said that he felt 'a little unwell' but after diving into the cold river he was 'fresh and well.'

The next day he met David Zeisberger who was with an Indian companion who also spoke English. While their horses ate grass, they talked, but as the Moravian missionary was in a hurry and 'travelling faster' they parted. The following day was heavy with rain so they stayed in their tents and Woolman did some more musing; this time regarding 'the nature of the exercise which hath attended me.' Why had he come into these parts to be with the natives? Considering the dangers of such a journey at this time, Woolman's answer to himself is extraordinary. He said:

> Love was the first motion, and then a concern arose to spend some time with the Indians, that I might feel and understand their life and the spirit they live in, if haply I might receive some instruction from them, or they be in any degree helped forward by my following the leadings of Truth amongst them.

This is a truly remarkable statement for the time; indeed for all time. Consider that most Europeans encountering the native Americans felt they were savages, barely human. And when a religious interest was shown to them, it was to convert them to true religion whether it be Catholic or Presbyterian or Moravian. Even Zeisberger – who did so much to help the natives – would never have said he 'might receive some instruction from them.' Woolman's simple expression speaks volumes – and is one of the things for which we love him today.

The sun was shining the next day so they were able to set out with little difficulty. As they proceeded, Woolman's thoughts returned to the plight of the Indians. As English settlements increased, natives 'for trifling considerations' were selling favourably situated lands. That pushed them to less desirable locales and they were also discovering that the animals upon which they had so heavily depended were becoming less plentiful. As always drink continued to be a major curse. Unlike others of his day, Woolman could see that the Indians' plight was similar to the state of Negro slavery and for both 'the seeds of great calamity and desolation are sown and growing fast on this continent.' This was 1762 and Woolman was witnessing only the tip of a hideous iceberg of what Stuart Wavell has termed 'The most shameful period of America's domestic history – the virtual extermination of the aboriginal population and the rape of their land, driven by naked greed.'[98]

When they reached Wyoming they were given news that Indians had taken an English fort and were on to another. Also in a town about ten miles to the north, Indian warriors 'from distant parts' had arrived with two English scalps telling them 'it was war with the English.'

With that news fresh in his ears, Woolman must have been startled by what transpired next. They were taken to the house of a very old Indian where they placed their luggage. Soon after, another Indian appeared with a tomahawk concealed under his coat. Woolman said it had a very 'disagreeable appearance,' and as Woolman approached him the Indian took the hatchet in his hand. But Woolman moved forward and spoke to him 'in a friendly way.' Parvin then entered the scene and they had 'some talk concerning the nature of our visit in these parts.' Apparently the Indian with the tomahawk was won over: he sat down and smoked his pipe. Later Woolman confided in his journal: 'I believe he had no other intent than to be in readiness in case any violence was offered him.' One can only imagine how John's wife felt when later she heard this account from her husband.

On 17th June, Woolman and his party reached Wyalusing in the middle of the afternoon. Woolman commented that he had been 'favoured with health as to continue travelling' but admitted being weary from the 'difficulties in our journey and different way of living' as well as the accounts that Indian warriors were on the march close by.

The Indians had been told of their coming and soon a conch shell was blown several times and Woolman and his party were invited into a house where like a Quaker Meeting sixty people sat in silence. After a short time Woolman stood up and expressed his greetings from the Friends and naively displayed his certificate from Monthly Meeting. He tried to explain what that indicated; doubtless it was something foreign to them. Wyalusing was a Moravian missionary community and Woolman does not refer to their leader by name. It probably was David Zeisberger whom they had encountered earlier on their journey. Anyway, Woolman was careful to note that 'the Indians, knowing that the Moravian and I were of different religious Societies' wanted no 'jarring or discord' in their meetings. In an ecumenical spirit Woolman spoke to the Moravian leader of his concern for the Indian community and asked for permission to speak to them. He desired no conflict of interests.

Translation must have been difficult. The primary language of the Moravians was still German and Woolman said that the interpreters at the gathering endeavored 'to acquaint the people with what I said,' but none of them 'was quite perfect in the English and Delaware tongue.' But despite this, Woolman made a favourable impression — especially with a remarkable old Indian named Papunehang. Woolman called him 'the man who had been zealous in labouring for a reformation in (Wyalusing).' Before his conversion by Zeisberger, Papunehang had been a religious leader of sorts — a bit like a medicine man — but after becoming a Moravian he had led an exemplary Christian life and was often referred to by travellers in the area. Though he did not understand the words Woolman used at the meeting, Papunehang was certainly aware of the spirit behind them; as he told an interpreter: 'I love to feel where words come from.'

Woolman and his party had several other meetings with the Indians, and after several days, felt 'at liberty to return' home. The return journey was easier as they joined some Indians on their way to Bethlehem with skins and furs. Woolman noted that the path between the English habitations and Wyalusing was quite narrow and 'much grown up with bushes and (an) abundance of trees.' There was also the persistent danger of rattlesnakes; Woolman said they killed four. How we long for more of those 'local colour' touches from him. Alas, that was never part of his concern in writing. At least, however, Woolman's words are more expressive than the dry minute which comes from Mount Holly Meeting upon his return:

> Ist of 8 mo. 1763. Our friend John Woolman being returned from his visit to some religiously disposed Indians up Susquehanna, informed the last meeting that he was treated kindly, and had satisfaction in his visit.

A few months later in the aftermath of the anti-Indian feeling, a new danger came to Philadelphia. A mob of Scotch-Irish entered Germantown led by the infamous 'Paxton boys' (several border ruffians). For long the ruffians had coveted the rich land around Conestoga near Lancaster where peaceful Mennonites had settled. Unsuccessfully the Paxtons had tried to get their hands on the unfarmed land. Now they took advantage of the anti-Indian sentiment.

At Conestoga lived twenty Christian Susquehannock Indians and more than half of them were old people and little children. They were the last of their nation. On 14 December 1763, during a snowfall, the Paxtons led by an hysterical elder of the Presbyterian church murdered six of the Susquehannocks. The remainder were quickly sent away by the authorities and placed in the supposed safety of a strongly built workhouse in Lancaster. Unopposed the Paxtons followed them and with axes hacked their way into the shelter and butchered them all.

John Penn, who was an eyewitness, gave this chilling account:

Those cruel men ... by violence broke open the (workhouse) door, and entered with the utmost fury ... When the poor wretches saw they had no protection ... nor could possibly escape, and being without the least weapon for defense ... they divided into their little families, the children clinging to the parents; they fell on their knees, protested their innocence, declared their love to the English, and that, in their whole lives, they had never done them injury; and in this posture they all received the hatchet! Men, women, and little children were every one inhumanely murdered! in cold blood! ... The bodies of the murdered were then brought out and exposed in the street, till a hole could be made in the earth, to receive and cover them.[99]

Word spread among other tribes near Conestoga. Some Indians George Logan wrote about, were taken to barracks not far from his home at Stenton, north of Philadelphia. Logan was ten at the time and his grandfather, James, had been the secretary and trusted friend of William Penn. The regiment of Highlanders stationed at the barracks refused to share their quarters with 'aborigines', so they were sent 'shivering with fear and cold' to islands in the Delaware River. Finally New York offered them a haven and it was William Logan (George's father) who travelled north with them. The experience had a great effect on young George who had been taught to accept Indians as 'fellow human beings'.

The Logans were not the only Quakers to be affected by the horror. Zeisberger's community at Wyalusing thought they should leave and seek safety in Philadelphia. Zeisberger agreed and when they arrived in Germantown on the outskirts of Philadelphia they were greeted by Israel Pemberton, Anthony Benezet and like-minded Friends. But close on their heels was the Paxton-led mob. Only a determined (and armed) group of Philadelphia citizens led by Benjamin Franklin persuaded them to leave Germantown.

By then, the December cold affected the unsheltered Indians and Israel Pemberton, William Logan and Woolman helped care for them in the barracks of Philadelphia. After some months they returned to Wyalusing. Ironically some of the Quaker meeting records displayed more concern with disciplining the Quakers who 'in the excitement of the hour and danger ... took up arms to back Franklin.'[100] Woolman did not refer to the event in the *Journal*, but as Janet Whitney says: 'This flurry may have been part of the reason why Woolman's family joined households with Asher's (his brother) that December.'[101]

A picture of Quakers and Indians less known than Benjamin West's is a sketch by James Doyle Penrose which portrays an event at Easton Township in New York's Saratoga County. In it an Indian chief arrives at a Quaker Meeting where Friends sit in silence. There are no guns with them, nothing they could use for protection. The Indians have noted the quiet, and a little boy turns to gaze at the proud chief with feathered headgear. The account upon which the sketch was based indicates that the Indians were as taken by surprise as the Quakers. But soon the Indians recognize what is going on: in silence the settlers have approached the Great Spirit. According to the story, afterwards the Indians joined the Friends for a meal and when they departed, they placed a white feather on the meeting house: a symbol that these people were their friends.

This simple work portrays the best in the Quaker association with the native Americans.

'Fierce Feathers' or 'None Shall Make Them Afraid'.

Superfluities and True Harmony

OFTEN WOOLMAN SPOKE of the frivolities of society, and though not as severe as the Puritans, the Quakers frowned on such pleasures as dancing, the theatre and the arts. It would be some time before the Quaker establishment of Philadelphia would take an interest in the arts, but there were always those 'gay Quakers' who risked the rebuke of the Society and shed Quaker grey, the uniform caps and broad-brimmed hats, and danced. Dolley Madison (the fourth President's wife), who was raised at the Quaker community of New Garden in North Carolina (even before she became the celebrated hostess in the White House) had discarded her Quaker dress and religion for Anglicanism. Apparently once she was taken back by the remark of a European traveller who commented that the beauty of Quaker girls was enhanced rather than diminished by their simple attire.

Ironically, though plain, some of the homes of the Quaker rich in Philadelphia, like the Logans' Stenton Mansion, used only the finest craftsmanship (always Quaker when it could be found) and the materials for their 'plain' clothing was of the very best quality. With increased prosperity came a gradual weakening of the Quaker objection to luxury. Some kept elegant coaches and liveried drivers. When Isaac Norris bought a new coach in 1713 even he could not bring himself to having a coat-of-arms painted on the door and settled for his initials; his coachman was dressed in something 'strong and cheap, either of a dark grey or sad colour.'

Despite these extraordinary superfluities, members of the Society continued to hold art in distrust and their Meeting Houses forever remained a testament to their plainness; always devoid of decoration. But even here – as the Shakers would discover – there was a further irony that the plain integrity of the meeting house

81

and wonderfully simple furniture would be viewed by outsiders as having a certain beauty and value in itself. This aesthetic appreciation is, however, latter-day when Quaker quarrels with the arts have gone. Today the Society has a number of distinguished actors and actresses and those involved in all the arts.

In the summer of 1763 a man we would identify as a magician or juggler came to Mount Holly. More than harmless to us, but in the early American severity, magic was attuned to the Devil. The magician presented an advertisement that he would perform in a public house. When Woolman saw this he had 'an exercise' in his mind. Again that wonderfully quaint word! Woolman went along to see what was transpiring and as people came into the pub he talked with them saying: 'those tricks or sleights-of-hand' they were willing to pay to see 'were of no use in the world,' and worse – 'contrary to the nature of the Christian religion.' Some of the people who gathered argued with him 'to show the reasonableness of (the) proceedings,' but after a while they gave up. And after an hour, so did Woolman. We have difficulties with this rather priggish aspect of Woolman, and generally speaking, one of the things we miss most in his writings is some sense of humour – or at least some occasional lightness of soul. However, it can be said that unlike the Calvinists, at least Woolman's approach in this event was quiet and low-key: friendly persuasion again.

Woolman was not the only Quaker disturbed by the effects of wealth in the Society of Friends. At Yearly Meeting in September 1764, 83-year-old John Smith voiced his concern. Smith was born in Massachusetts and at 22 was imprisoned for his testimony against war. Two years later, he went to England where he was 'pressed' on board a man-of-war and imprisoned again; this time for six weeks. Upon returning to America, he married and lived forty years in East Marlborough, Pennsylvania, where for a long time Friends meetings gathered at his home.

Woolman referred to him as 'a faithful minister though not eloquent.' In the meeting of ministers and elders he stood up and 'appearing to be under a great exercise of spirit' he said that for more than sixty years he had been a member of the Society and remembered what 'plain, lowly-minded people' Friends used to be. But for twenty years or so they seemed to be 'conforming to the fashions of the world,' becoming very rich, wearing costly garments, using silver and the rest. Old Smith would die three years after that.

Woolman kept up a lively pace visiting Friends who continued to keep slaves and in October 1765, he felt drawn to the eastern shores of Maryland and over to Delaware. It was at that time he encountered followers of Joseph Nichols whom he described as 'not in outward fellowship with any religious Society of people, but professeth nearly the same principles as our Society doth.'

Nichols was born in Delaware about 1730 and like Woolman died shortly before the outbreak of the American War of Independence. Also like Woolman he came from a farming background and practised husbandry near Dover in Delaware. Apparently Nichols was greatly influenced by Quakerism but developed his own peculiar views among his companions. Like the Quakers they held meetings in silence, but Nichols, a powerful speaker, often preached. There remains little specific information about his gatherings, but it is known the Nicholites had testimonies against war, oaths and a paid clergy.

Woolman noted 'Some irregularities, I hear, have been amongst the people at several of his meetings', but we know no more than that. In 1778, some of Nichols' followers migrated to North Carolina where they soon joined the Quaker fellowship. Nicholites were consistent in their testimony against slavery and it appears that Negroes were freely accepted at their meetings. Even more striking in relation to John Woolman, was that Nicholites adopted undyed clothing as a sort of uniform garb, but there is no evidence that this was the case when Woolman visited them. They were also strongly against all ornaments in clothing; a bit like the Mennonites. It has been speculated by Kenneth Carroll and others that perhaps Woolman had a considerable influence among them during his visit, but we do not know whether he met Nichols or not.[102] By the end of the 18th-century, the Nicholites had merged within the Society of Friends, and they remain today as a curious footnote in American religious history.

During these visits in eastern Maryland, Woolman made some interesting observations on the 'different circumstances' of Quakers in Pennsylvania and New Jersey from those in the southern colonies. It is an 'overview' not many of his time would see. But Woolman had travelled far and wide and could see that those Friends who 'were convinced of our principles in England in times of suffering' had bought lands of the natives and 'applied themselves to husbandry in a peaceful way.' Friends who later settled to the south were not as grounded in the ideals of Penn's holy experiment and were vastly outnumbered by other settlers with views quite different from the Quaker. As Richard Middleton has put it: '... only the Quakers attempted to treat the American Indians as equal,' and 'this same egalitarianism was leading them to denounce slavery as well.'[103]

No such compunction swayed the Scotch-Irish as we have seen. As Middleton continues: 'For them the American Indian was a heathen outside the moral law,'[104] and they with other religionists extended this to the Blacks as well. This variance cannot be overstressed and accounts for the long long time it would take for views now accepted as 'American' to take root. The Quakers paid a price for their early tolerance and understanding of both native and African Americans. Woolman was near to seeing this overriding problem but, basically his experience was within Quaker limitations and we wonder just how aware he was of the degree of variance held among religious groups then pouring into the colonies.

Calvinists – as we have noted – viewed the Blacks as sons of Cain, and the Indians were equated with the detested Amalekites of the Bible. They even found texts to justify slaying the natives and taking their land. The Amalekites were the descendants of Esau and from the time of the Exodus a constant plague to the Israelites. Saul 'cut the Amalekites to pieces' and a final blow was struck against them by King David.[105] Upon what basis the poor Indians were identified as Amalekites one can only imagine. But equally farfetched was the notion by William Penn (and much later the Mormons) that the Indians were the lost tribes of Israel.

But there was more to the matter than just bizarre usage of Scripture. There was a basic philosophical divide between Calvinists and Quakers. As Richard Middleton says it is a point often overlooked by historians: '... Quakers believed that people were intrinsically good and needed only marginal direction. This view was the exact opposite of the Puritan concept of human depravity.'[106]

Woolman displayed this well; he was never deterred from a generous optimism that eventually all men could change: '... some of these (slave) masters I suppose are awakened to feel and see their error and through sincere repentance cease from oppression and become like fathers to their servants ...'

It would be some time before such optimism would appear among the children of the Puritans and Scotch-Irish Presbyterians, but in the next century Unitarianism and Universalism would make inroads into the Puritan heartland and members of the Congregationalist and Presbyterian churches would be in the vanguard of abolitionism. Sadly, healthier attitudes toward the native Americans would come too late.

During the years 1766 to 1768, Woolman made several journeys, many alone and all on foot. From the visit into Delaware and the eastern shore of Maryland, he went into upper New Jersey and then into the western part of Maryland and in 1768 he spent five weeks in Maryland again. Increasingly he spoke of his 'bodily weakness' and 'a heavy exercising mind.' But he said that his sufferings were little compared with the slaves with whom he identified, and more and more he linked their suffering with that of Christ and the early Christian martyrs. It is here that we note Woolman's affinity with Christian mystics like John of the Cross and Teresa of Avila. However, Woolman's 'suffering for Christ' was not for saintly enlightenment: it was sharing in the oppression of the slaves.

The Moravians, whom Woolman well knew, also meditated upon the sufferings of Christ, but in a manner Woolman would have found abhorrent: their emphasis on the atoning death of Christ 'turned in a distorted direction, focusing on a morbid concentration and wordplay upon the blood and wounds of the crucified Christ.'[107]

For long Woolman had felt that he should 'make some restitution' for the gain he had made long ago when he kept shop and retailed rum, sugar and molasses; products of slave labour. He considered a voyage to Barbados – but it was a trip he would not make. There was the family to consider and the obvious problem of whether it was right for him to travel on a ship engaged in the slave trade, as most ships to Barbados were. But something else intervened as well: illness. On 12 March 1770 Woolman said 'Having for some years past dieted myself on account of a lump on my nose, and under the diet grew weak in body and not of ability to travel by land as heretofore.' Worse was to come: pleurisy, an inflammation of the membrane enveloping the lungs.

It is now known that pleurisy can be caused by bacterial or viral infection and can easily be treated with antibiotics. Accompanying it is a fever and a pain in the chest that becomes worse on coughing or taking a deep breath. In Woolman's day it was quite serious, and he 'felt the disorder very grievous' and thought 'how it might end.'

During the worst stage of his illness Woolman had the second vision he recorded in his journal, but he did not mention it until he was in England, two and a half years later. He said: 'I was brought so near the gates of death I forgot my name.' Wanting to know who he was he saw 'a mass of matter of a dull gloomy colour' and was informed that the mass 'was human beings in as great misery as they could be and live, and that I was mixed in with them and henceforth might not consider myself as a distinct or separate being.'

Woolman remained in that condition several hours and then heard 'a soft, melodious voice, more pure and harmonious than any voice I had heard with my ears before and I believed it was the voice of an angel.' The angel said: '*John Woolman is dead.*' Woolman said he remembered he was once John Woolman and wondered what the voice could mean. It was 'a mystery' he recalled and 'a case uncommon.'

Uncommon indeed for Woolman as we have seen, for he was not much given to visions. This account has been interpreted in varying fashion over the years. Elton Trueblood says it reminds him of the words of John Donne's famous sermon:

No man is an island, entire of itself; every man is a piece of the continent, a part of the main ... Any man's death diminishes me, because I am involved in mankind; And therefore never send to know for whom the bell tolls; It tolls for thee.[108]

John Lampen was reminded of words from Carl Jung during a turning point in his life:

When I look back on it all today ... it seems as though a message had come to me with overwhelming force. There were things in the images which concerned not only myself but many others also. It was then that I ceased to belong to myself, alone, ceased to have the right to do so.[109]

Woolman himself said that the following morning he suddenly understood what 'John Woolman is dead' meant: 'no more than the death of my own will.' Earlier and in the presence of his wife and others he had quoted Paul's words in Galatians 2.20: 'I am crucified with Christ, nevertheless I live; yet not I, but Christ that liveth in me, and the life I now live in the flesh is by faith in the Son of God, who loved me and gave himself for me.'

The vision affected Woolman greatly: apparently he signed the account with his name in his manuscript and referred to it as a 'dispensation', a word associated with experiences of saints and mystics. Woolman also said that after his sickness and vision he did not speak (minister) in public meetings for worship for nearly a year. His mind was occupied 'with the oppressed slaves as I sat in meetings.'

Later in 1770 John Woolman recovered from pleurisy and it is that point that the American section of his journal ends. During that year he revised and rewrote his work preparing it for eventual publication. He also quietly occupied himself at home, taking care of his fruit trees and overseeing the building of a house in Mount Holly for his daughter, Mary, as the next year she was to marry John Comfort who had been learning orcharding from John Woolman. Comfort was the eldest of the nine children of Stephen and Mercy Comfort of Middletown in Bucks County. As Janet Whitney put it: 'In literal truth John Woolman had gained a son rather than lost a daughter.'[110]

Woolman also had been busy with other writing: remarkable considering the travelling he had accomplished. But somehow he always seemed to find time. It is thought that soon after his journey to the Indians at Wyalusing he had composed much of *A Plea for the Poor*, which was to become one of his most cited essays. It was not published until 1793, and almost a hundred years later the Fabian Society in England reprinted it as one of its tracts. The socialist society was founded in 1884 and George Bernard Shaw was one of its members. It generally advocated social change through gradual reforms rather than by violent revolutionary actions associated with other socialist groups of the time. One need go no further than the opening paragraph of *A Plea for the Poor* to see why socialists would find it appealing:

> Wealth desired for its own sake obstructs the increase of virtue, and large possessions in the hands of selfish men have a bad tendency, for by their means too small a number of people are employed in things useful; and therefore they, or some of them, are necessitated to labour too hard, while others would want business to earn their bread were not employments invented which, having no real use, serve only to please the vain mind.[111]

Phillips Moulton tells us that the sixteenth chapter of the essay generally omitted when it was published 'includes a penetrating analysis of the exploitation of black slaves by their white masters (even when the latter had good intentions)'. Interestingly, the sixteenth chapter

> concludes with a cogent case for the payment of reparations to the descendants of these mistreated members of our society, thus dealing directly with the issue raised so forcibly in the Black Manifesto of 1969.[112]

There were some very practical points in Woolman's essay: he was among the first to point out the disadvantage of large classes in schools. Like other Quakers (some of them quite wealthy), he was against leaving great estates for offspring: 'To treasure up wealth for another generation ... is doing evil at present without knowing ...'[113] Woolman also believed: '... many ... would embrace a way of life less expensive and lighten the heavy burdens of some who now labour out of their sight to support them.'[114]

As ever Woolman's concern extended to all creation and he noted the oppression of oxen and horses through over-working:

Oxen and horses are often seen at work when, through heat and too much labour, their eyes and the emotion of their bodies manifest that they are oppressed. Their loads in wagons are frequently so heavy that when weary with hauling it far, their drivers find occasion in going up hills or through mire to raise their spirits by whipping to get forward. Many poor people are so thronged in their business that it is difficult for them to provide shelter suitable for their animals in great storms.[115]

All fitted together in one design and Reginald Reynolds ended *The Wisdom of John Woolman* with a passage from *A Plea for the Poor* which he calls 'one of the most beautiful and comprehensive passages in all Woolman's writings, in which the Seed, the Flower, and the Fruit appear at a single glance':[116]

Our Gracious Creator cares and provides for all his Creatures. His tender mercies are over all his works; and, so far as his love influences our minds, so far we become interested in his workmanship, and feel a desire to take hold of every opportunity to lessen the distresses of the afflicted and increase the happiness of the Creation. Here we have a prospect of one common interest, from which our own is inseparable, that to turn all the treasures we possess into the channel of Universal Love becomes the business of our lives.[117]

Sometime in 1768 (the year Woolman journeyed on foot, alone, into Maryland for five weeks) *Considerations on Pure Wisdom and Human Policy* was published and *Considerations on the True Harmony of Mankind* in 1770, the year of his pleurisy. In the latter work, Woolman in another remarkably prophetic manner spoke of the corruptions of city life:

The condition of many who dwell in cities hath often affected me with a brotherly sympathy, attended with a desire that resignation may be laboured for; and where the Holy Leader directeth to a country life, or some change of employ, he may be faithfully followed. For, under the refining hand of the Lord, I have seen that the inhabitants of some cities are greatly increased through some branches of business which his Holy

Spirit doth not lead into; and that being entangled in these things tends to bring a cloud over the minds of people convinced of the leadings of this Holy Leader, and obstructs the coming of the kingdom of Christ on earth ...[118]

Conversations on the True Harmony of Mankind was composed in 1772 before Woolman left for England. It was not published, however, until 1837. In it Woolman struck what today we would call an environmental note:

Sheep are pleasant company on a plantation, their looks are modest, their voice is soft and agreeable; their defenceless state exposeth them a prey to wild beasts, and they appear to be intended by the great Creator to live under our protection, and supply us with matter for warmth and useful clothing. Sheep being rightly managed tend to enrich our land; but by sending abroad great quantities of grain and flour the fatness of our land is diminished.

I have known landowners who paid interest for large sums of money, and, being intent on paying their debts by raising grain, have too much tilling so robbed the earth of its natural fatness that the produce thereof hath grown light.

To till poor land requires near as much labour as to till that which is rich; and, as the high interest of money which lieth on many husbandmen is often a means for their struggling for present profit, to the impoverishment of their lands, they then on their poor land find greater difficulty to afford poor labourers, who work for them, equitable pay for tilling the ground.

The produce of the earth is a gift from our gracious Creator to the inhabitants, and to impoverish the earth now to support outward greatness appears to be an injury to the succeeding age.[119]

strengthned with his Love, and kept inwardly waiting for his Consil —

This afternoon Saw that part of England called the Lizard, and with a pleasant breafe of wind Stood our course, and Saild along in plain sight of the Green fields before night

Some dunghill fouls yet remained alive, of those which the pasengers took for eating on the way, — I believe about 14 perished in the Storms, at Sea, and I believe near as many died with

A page from Woolman's Journal at sea approaching England, 1772.
Courtesy the Library Friends House, London.

91

PART FOUR

The Longest Journey of His Life

WE DO NOT KNOW exactly when John Woolman decided to take on the longest journey of his life – and his last. It certainly appears to have been in his mind by 1771 as his daughter Mary and her husband John Comfort were settled in their home. Janet Whitney makes a point of the fact that 'he paid for all the materials and labour in the building of Mary's house with cash.'[120] From Woolman's account books of the time it is also apparent that he had not planned any long-term future engagements in surveying, teaching or legal work.

Some have noted an influence from Samuel Neale for Woolman to make a journey to England. Neale, a noted Irish Friend, visited New Jersey in the summer of 1771 and one author maintains that Woolman's conversations with Neale 'made Woolman feel without any doubt that he had to go.'[121] But we have no account of these conversations; only Neale's charming diary entries of meeting Woolman:

> 7th mo, 23rd, 1771. I was at Rancocas meeting ... Here I saw John Woolman for the first time. I take him to be a sweet, clean-spirited Friend; his unity with the true Seed may be felt by his savory conversation and ... self denying life.

The next day Neale went to Mount Holly Meeting and said:

> Pomp and splendour he avoids, does not choose to use silver or useless vessels ... his house is very plain, his living so also; and yet he enjoys plenty of the good things that are necessary for Christian accommodation.[122]

Probably more significant were the earlier visits of two English women: Jane Crosfield and Rachel Wilson. Jane Crosfield grew up near Swarthmoor in what Friends call 1652 country (the early centres of Quakerism near and around the Lake District). In 1760, she made a visit to Philadelphia and became well acquainted with Woolman. Rachel Wilson from Kendal (in the Lake District) was a prominent Quaker, and in 1768 and 1769 she travelled on horse-back through the American colonies. In 1769, she also attended Philadelphia Yearly Meeting and during a sermon when she was about to speak of her own activities, she stopped and addressed herself directly to John Woolman who at the time was agonizing over his proposed visit to Barbados:

> She addressed him with much sympathy; and ardently wished the good hand might be with him, and enable him to divide the word aright, to the honour of the great name, the comfort of those among whom he had to labour, and his own everlasting peace.[123]

An interesting letter dated 1 January 1772, survives from Joseph Oxley of Norwich. After discussing the proposed visit to Britain of a Philadelphia Friend, Oxley wrote:

> ... another Friend, John Woolman, a wise sensible man having a good gift in the ministry and well approved of, has a concern of the like kind more particularly to Yorkshire. I suppose the latter will hardly leave the continent till the summer.[124]

By April Woolman had written a deed of trust which would serve in case of death as a will. He left his property in the hands of John Comfort's father who would act as the executor. The deed would turn out to be the only will Woolman made. Certainly in the back of his mind was the fact that a grandchild was expected (a grandson, John, was born 20th June). Woolman also gave the manuscript of his journal, his last essays, and an Epistle to be circulated among Friends to John Pemberton who would act as a literary executor of sorts.

It would appear that for long Woolman had desired to take his concern over slavery to England – and to the London Yearly Meeting. There remains a curious bit of evidence for this. Henry Cadbury has noted the account of a dream once intended as part of the *Journal*. The account is dated 26 July 1764 and begins: 'At night I dreamed I was abroad on a religious visit beyond the sea, and had been out upward of two months ...' Cadbury feels that this gives some indication of 'how long this anticipation had been in or beneath (Woolman's) consciousness.'[125]

There was also another dream: this one like a premonition of a future visit. It was of uncertain date and was recorded from Woolman's deathbed at York:

He (Woolman) had long had a view of visiting this nation, and some time before he came had a dream, in which he saw himself in the northern parts of it; and that the spring of the gospel was opened in him, much as in the beginning of Friends such as George Fox and William Dewsbury; and he saw the different states of the people as clear as he had ever seen flowers in a garden; but in his going on, he was suddenly stopt, though he could not see for what end; but looked towards home and thereupon fell into a flood of tears which waked him.[126]

In April, as he intended to visit chiefly the northern parts of England, Woolman looked for a ship bound for Liverpool or Whitehaven. But while in Philadelphia he learned that his friend, Samuel Emlen, had already secured passage in the *Mary & Elizabeth* bound for London. That changed his mind.

Samuel Emlen (1730-1799) was raised in a wealthy Philadelphia household; slight and delicate of frame, like Woolman, he was never very robust. But he was well educated and spoke modern languages fluently, and the ancient ones of Greek and Latin as well. It is recorded that once he addressed a learned audience for an hour in Latin. For a time he was employed in the counting house of James Pemberton, but his poor eyesight plus an inherited fortune, led him to leave full-time business pursuits. He travelled through the southern colonies and probably kept Woolman informed of the condition of slaves in the Deep South. Emlen also visited Britain several times – travelling in the ministry – and could well advise Woolman on such matters.

The two visited the *Mary & Elizabeth* together: it was a custom of travelling Quakers to go on board a potential vessel to get a 'feel' of whether the ship was the right one or not. Emlen was well accustomed to doing this but not prepared for Woolman's reaction. Emlen's cabin was comfortable and well ornamented; Woolman did not want that for himself. After visiting the sailors' quarters and steerage accommodation and noting the stark simplicity, Woolman

94

made his choice. The *Mary & Elizabeth* was owned by John Head, a Quaker, but one not used to the likes of Woolman. His choice of steerage created a fuss and Emlen wept when he realized what Woolman intended to do. Israel Pemberton tried to change Woolman's mind stressing 'the great inconvenience of steerage.' Later, Israel's brothers accompanied Woolman to the ship to dissuade him as well, and Emlen took Woolman to John Head's house. There Woolman told Head he 'felt a scruple' paying the extra money involved with a cabin and its unnecessary trimmings. But soon the stronger reason surfaced. Woolman said: 'I was now desirous to embrace every opportunity of being inwardly acquainted with the hardship and difficulties of my fellow creatures ...' Certainly in the back of his mind was how those whom he championed had made their awful passage from Africa.

Before he left for Philadelphia and the sailing, Woolman visited Joseph White who 'had a mind to see me.' White of Bucks County was apparently close to Woolman and had an interesting history: orphaned, at age 20 he began to preach and spent three years in England. Woolman did not say in his *Journal* what they discussed but the next day he was back home and spent the next two nights there.

Customarily Woolman said little about what would turn out to be his last time with his family; only the words: 'And then early in the morning I parted with my family under a sense of the humbling hand of God upon me.' In his usual thorough manner, Henry Cadbury goes through the surviving records and gives an interesting anecdote from John Cox of Burlington (1754?-1847):

John Woolman's widow used to come and spend several days at a time with us, and delighted to talk of Johnny as she frequently called him. When he was about to embark for Europe he went to Philadelphia to look at the ship to see whether he would feel easy to embark in her. He finally felt satisfied to engage his passage in the steerage *conditionally* – and if he felt easy after reaching home would come again to the City in time for the sailing of the vessel. He went to bed as usual in Mount Holly – and in the morning when his wife awakened she missed him, and supposing he was making ready to depart went downstairs, but finding him gone she went into the road in search of him, and ascertained from one of the neighbours that he had seen him about daylight with a bundle under his arm going on foot towards Philadelphia. His wife never saw him afterwards, for he embarked on shipboard and ended his valuable life while on religious service in England.[127]

Cadbury says 'The account was criticized when thus published, ostensibly because it was felt to conflict with that in the *Journal* but actually I think because it seemed "an unceremonious departure" for John Woolman.'[128] Janet Whitney must have known the account as she added to what comes from the *Journal* that Woolman would not wake his wife 'even with a kiss to the mutual anguish of another parting.'[129] Actually Cox's account appears in keeping with Woolman's behaviour regarding his family and earlier departings: the agonizing when he left for Wyalusing to visit the Indians, a case in point. It was understandable for a man so driven by duty, as well as so sensitive to others, not to inflict any more pain than was already present. One thing seems certain: by this time – after twenty-three years of marriage – Sarah Woolman was accustomed to Johnny's unusual nature, singularities and unswaying convictions. We might have difficulties with the seeming coldness of such a departure; probably Sarah well understood the reasons behind it.

The *Mary & Elizabeth's* company numbered about 30 and Woolman knew a number of the passengers. Other than Emlen, there was the young widow of William Logan, Jr, returning home to England with a small son and a maid. Samuel Emlen and Dr John Till Adams were her escorts. Another passenger, John Bispham, was a neighbour at Mount Holly and only twenty years old. He was the son of Joseph Bispham, and his uncle was also named John Bispham. As Henry Cadbury suggested in 1971, for long, biographers (and at first Cadbury as well) thought that John Bispham, Sr (1734-1791) was Woolman's shipmate. Cadbury well proves otherwise and it was the young man who later would be with Woolman in London and also sent for, when Woolman was dying in York.

Woolman had not long been at sea when he took pity on the seamen, many of them young lads; among them two had been raised as Quakers. As Amelia Gummere says:

Although it is probable that the sailors on this ship under Capt. Sparks were superior to the average seamen of the eighteenth century, as they are described by Defoe and Smollett, nevertheless their surroundings were unspeakably bad, and their habits were coarse and brutal beyond belief.[130]

Not only did Woolman live among them, he talked with them and gained their confidence. In a fashion they were his 'charge' and – as always – he sought to teach them a regard for their fellow creatures. One lad was James Nayler and his father's uncle was the famous James Nayler (c.1618-1660), one of the most prominent early Friends.

Whereas most of his fellow passengers became seasick, Woolman did not: 'through the tender mercies of my Heavenly Father I have been spared.' He added that his 'afflictions' were 'of another kind.' That was, of course, what he observed concerning the young seamen aboard: 'How great is that danger to which poor lads are now exposed when placed on shipboard to learn the art of sailing.' Their watch was four hours at a time: especially grim when it was both dark and rainy. There was little room to rest and their clothing was almost always damp. When it was discarded it was thrown in a large smelly bundle right in the middle of steerage.

The wonder is that Woolman survived as well as he did, but about a week out at sea, he said that the wind was so vehement he spent seventeen hours up in the cabins of friends. He well described a scene at night during a particularly awful storm: '... the sea wrought exceedingly and the high foaming waves all round about had in some sort the appearance of fire, but did not give much if any light.'

Woolman said he had

frequent opportunities of hearing conversation amongst the sailors in respect to the voyages to Africa and the manner of bringing the deeply oppressed slaves into our islands, the thoughts of their condition, frequently in chains and fetters, on board the vessels, with hearts loaded with grief under the apprehension of miserable slavery ...

He meditated on those things realizing that even his and the sailors' miserable steerage offered an advantage not available to the slaves:

he and the sailors could always get up and walk the deck and breath some fresh air.

Seventeen days into the trip Woolman admitted being home-sick: 'a tender sympathy of soul with my poor wife and family left behind.' A week later he said that shut up below in 'close, unhealthy air' he felt weak and 'Several nights of late I felt breathing difficult.' But going on deck seemed to revive him.

On the second of June, they sighted Lizard Point in Cornwall and it was then that Woolman turned his attention where few men would – to the fowls which remained from those brought on board for the passengers. Fourteen of the birds had perished in the storms at sea when waves broke over the quarter deck. Most had been sick at different times and Woolman remembered how the cocks among them crowed when they went down the Delaware River from Philadelphia. They had not crowed since but near land they did so again. In the *Journal* the event caused Woolman to record another of those remarkable statements which have come to be a part of all anthologies of those who have concern for animals:

Gracechurch Street Meeting in East London, circa 1770.
Courtesy the Library Friends House, London.

98

In observing their dull appearance at sea and the pining sickness of some of them, I often remembered the Fountain of Goodness, who gave being to all creatures, and whose love extends to that of caring for the sparrows; and (I) believe where the love of God is verily perfected and the true spirit of government watchfully attended to, a tenderness toward all creatures made subject to us will be experienced, and a care felt in us that we do not lessen that sweetness of life in the animal creation which the great Creator intends for them under our government ...

About noon on the fourth of June a pilot came off from Dover where Samuel Emlen went on shore. From there he would proceed to London and Yearly Meeting. Woolman, however, 'felt easy in staying in the ship' – staying until the next day when the *Mary & Elizabeth* arrived at the London docks.

Hertford Meeting House (see page 107).
Courtesy the Library Friends House, London.

A Season of Silence

CHAPTERS XI AND XII of Moulton's edition of the *Journal* comprise Woolman's account of his voyage to, and his time in England. The final version of this record in Woolman's own hand is kept at Swarthmore College in Pennsylvania and is seventy pages measuring 4 x 6½ inches all stitched together.

The final chapter (Chapter XII) began '8th day, 6th month, 1772.' He said that he 'Landed at London and went straitway to the Yearly Meeting ... which had been gathered about (I suppose) half an hour. In this meeting my mind was humbly contrite ...' Then he added a little about the afternoon meeting of business and several meetings for worship but that is all we have of Yearly Meeting. The next notation from Woolman has him in Hertford. We must look elsewhere for accounts of the effect Woolman had on the heart of Quakerdom.

Henry Cadbury tells us what a 'formidable undertaking' attendance at London Yearly Meeting was. For male Friends there were not only seven business sessions but also four sessions for ministers and elders. The women had only two business sessions, but all of this occurred within a week-long series of meetings for worship at various Meeting Houses. The business sessions were at Devonshire House which until 1925 served as the Quakers' London headquarters.

Woolman, of course, carried certificates from his monthly meeting and was well known to a number of English Friends. Despite this, his attire created a stir among some Quakers:

> a white hat, a coarse raw linen shirt, without anything about his neck, his coat, waistcoat and breeches of white coarse woolen cloth ... his coat without cuffs, white yarn stockings,

100

and shoes of uncured leather with bands instead of buckles, so that he was all white.[131]

A veritable apparition.

There are many dramatic accounts of Woolman's entry into Devonshire House before English Quakers in 'neat suits of excellent material, and cut-buff or brown or black or grey – with knee breeches and buckled shoes, and spotless linen at neck and wrist.'[132] One apocryphal American scenario (once used at the John Woolman Memorial in Mount Holly) goes as far as asserting: 'His white clothing had suffered considerably on the voyage and arriving at London Meeting, a superior English woman said to him, "Yankee, I think you should go back to the colonies."'[133]

As Cadbury says: these tales have become 'favourite(s) among Friends since.'[134] But getting to the reality of reactions is another matter. First of all, it should be noted that London Yearly Meeting was used to dealing with itinerant enthusiasts who appeared off the streets and the first reaction of some was that here was yet another one.

Henry Cadbury discovered that the first known version of Woolman's arrival at Devonshire House was said to be 'from the verbal tradition of the late Rebecca Jones,' the same Rebecca Jones we met earlier in the dealings with schools she, Anthony Benezet and Woolman operated. Some of that account is worth repeating:

This simple disciple, arriving late in the meeting, unannounced, and very peculiar in his appearance, was likely, at first sight, to be regarded as some itinerant enthusiast. His certificate was presented and read, when some one remarked, that perhaps the dedication of the Friend might be accepted, and he might feel himself easy to return to his native land. John Woolman entered into the closet of his heart, there to seek, in meekness of wisdom, instruction from his safe Counsellor. No feeling of resentment prevailed; but, conscious that the spirits of the prophets, are subject to the prophets, he was humbled and deeply affected by the want of the unity of the brethren, and his tears flowed freely. In the constraining love of Christ, and in love for his church and people, he had, at costly sacrifice, taken his life in his hands, and left behind him his home and its endearments ... He rose with meekness, and stated that he did not feel any release from his prospect, but he could not travel in Truth's service without the unity of his Friends, and that, while this was witheld, he should not be easy to be at any cost to them; that he was acquainted with the trades of a tailor and a shoemaker, and that he hoped while the impediment continued to be felt, Friends would be kindly willing to employ him in such business as he was capable of, that he might not be chargeable to any.

A season of silence ensued, during which tears flowed freely from many eyes. After a time, in the pure openings of truth, John Woolman spoke a few words in the ministry, in which capacity his voice had not, till that moment, been heard in Great Britain ... All obstruction was removed, and the flow of unity (first expressed by the Friend who had before spoken his doubts) became 'a river to swim in' ...[135]

Cadbury says that 'This account need not be distrusted even if we do not know its exact origin,' but he notes that 'Woolman ever being a shoemaker', was, of course, very doubtful.[136] John Fothergill wrote his brother, Samuel, 9 June 1772:

The affairs of the Meeting go on well. The Americans help us much. John Woolman is solid and weighty in his remarks. I wish he could be cured of some singularities but his real worth outweighs the husk.[137]

Janet Whitney suggests that John Fothergill was the Friend who first spoke against and then in favour of Woolman's concern to visit England, but as Cadbury says, 'Why ... I do not know.'[138] It was an unfortunate assumption which has led to other fabrications.

Oddly in hindsight, of the two men – Woolman and Fothergill – today it would probably be the latter who would seem the more bizarre as we see in a description from Fothergill's nephew:

(Dr John Fothergill) usually wore a low three-cornered hat; a white medical wig, with rows of small curls descending one under another from nearly white superfine cloth, the coat without any collar, large cuffs, and two of the buttons buttoned over his breast; the waistcoat with long flaps; the ends of his cravat were buttoned within his waistcoat; the stockings he wore were silk and the colour of his clothes; his buckles were small.[139]

102

In 1848, Nathan Kite attributed to Woolman himself the proposal to return to America:

> Finding his way somewhat closed, he meekly intimated that if Friends were uneasy with him he would return home ... His meekness made a favourable impression on all, and those who were dissatisfied with his dress were not willing to take the responsibility of preventing the fulfillment of Gospel mission. They withdrew all objections ...[140]

Most objections quickly passed as we see in the diary of Elihu Robinson from 1772:

> Our Friend John Woolman from Jersey made some pertinent remarks in this Meeting as in many others, and though the singularity of his appearance might in some meetings draw the attention of the youth, and even cause a change of countenance in some, yet the simplicity, solidity and clearness of his remarks made all these vanish, as mists at the sun's rising ...[141]

Another matter of confusion concerns the epistles on the issue of slavery by London Yearly Meeting. Like others, Whitney declares that the 1772 Epistle was 'the first public utterance of the London Yearly Meeting on slavery.'[142] However, Cadbury indicates that public utterances against slavery occurred in the Epistle of 1758 (known to Woolman) and that of 1763 as well. Furthermore, 'In 1772 and afterwards it was in almost every Epistle.'[143] This in no way detracts from Woolman's influence in 1772; with him the concern deepened and broadened.

Woolman's stay in London was brief and his host was John Townsend, a pewterer. He was modest but well respected, and curiously, Townsend made 'Guinea basins' for the African slave trade as well as the army and navy, 'reasoning that these people had to be fed.' But at least one of his apprentices refused to make the basins intended for the Guinea coast. Townsend lived at Prescot Street, Goodman's Fields, and after Woolman's death he visited Sarah Woolman. Amusingly he also suffered rebuke for an article of his attire: a red-spotted handkerchief about his neck!

In a letter to Sarah Woolman 9 November 1722, Townsend said:

He lodged at my house in London. His company and self-denying example were truly profitable to me and family ... He divers times told me that he had not had the smallpox and desired I would tell Friends that was the reason why he did not go to their houses. But if he was spared to return again to this city he believed he should have liberty to visit them. He frequently said he was resigned to the will of Providence. He was not afraid of the disorder, and if he catch'd it in going to meetings and in the way of his duty he should have no cause to reflect upon himself.[144]

Townsend had been chosen as Woolman's host in London by John Pemberton as we learn from the latter's correspondence to Joseph Row, 28 April 1772:

This goes per Capt. Sparks with whom our dear Friends John Woolman and Samuel Emlen embarks ... The first is a truly upright man but walks in a straiter path than some other good folks are led, or do travel in. He is a good minister, a sensible man, and though he may appear singular, yet from a close knowledge of him he will be found to be a man of sweet, clean spirit and preserved from harsh censure of those who do not see and conform as he does. It will be safest for Friends with you to leave him to his own feelings, and to walk and steer in that path which proves most easy to him, without using much arguments or persuasion. He will do nothing knowingly against the Truth, and has had long experience in the Truth. He is much beloved and respected among us, and I doubt not will on close acquaintance be so to the truly religious with you. I have recommended him to thy house or John Townsend's ...[145]

In another letter to Joseph Row (written more than a week after Woolman's death) Pemberton said:

If our dear Friend, J.W. is singular and walks in a manner no doubt in a cross to nature, yet how many are there whose demeanor, etc. is opposite to the simplicity of the Gospel, and perhaps his appearance may excite thoughts in some such ... I love him and desire his preservation.[146]

Townsend was responsible for forwarding correspondence between Woolman and his family and was told by Woolman he did not want to use the post coaches as he had learned that the speed employed was cruel both to the boys involved and the horses used. Woolman called them 'flying coaches'; 'those coaches which run so fast as oft to oppress the horses.' This scruple probably was why Woolman did not take the coach from Dover with Samuel Emlen.

Before Woolman left London he copied his Sea Journal and gave it to Sophia Hume, the great-granddaughter of Mary Fisher, one of the two Quakers first to go to Massachusetts and the author of a number of pamphlets known to Woolman. In America she made her home with Israel Pemberton. Woolman also wrote several letters home to America which survive. One was to his wife and said in part:

> My heart hath been often melted into contrition since I left thee, under a sense of divine goodness being extended for my help and preparing in me a subjection to his will ... I have often remembered you with tears ...

He also told Sarah that he had 'thoughts of going in a few days out of this city towards Yorkshire: taking some meetings in my way.'[147]

That last bit was an understatement. Unlike other American Quakers, Woolman took in few social gatherings over the 122 days in England, but up from London through the Midlands and into the Northern counties Woolman attended various meetings; from 15 June to 1 July alone he attended, in turn, Quarterly Meetings in five counties.

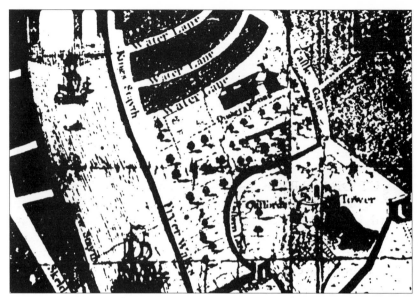

Enlargement of John Cossins' map of York 1727.

Sketch of York Quaker Meeting in 'Water Lane' by John Cossins, circa 1726. This is probably the earliest representation of the Meeting House built in 1718 to replace the original building.

These drawings are courtesy of Hugh Murray's Scarborough, York and Leeds: *the Town Plans of John Cossins 1697-1743, published by the Yorkshire Architectural and York Archaeological Society in 1997.*

York Looks Like Home

O UT OF LONDON Woolman's first stop was Hertford with
Quarterly Meeting on the 16th and 17th June. The old
records kept at the County Record Office say that he and two other
Americans (William Hunt and Thomas Thornburgh) were present
'in the course of their religious visits to this Island, their company
and labour of love was likewise greatly to our comfort and satisfaction.'[148] Hertford Meeting House, 'the oldest surviving Quaker
Meeting House to be built for the purpose in the world', is one of
the very few Meeting Houses left in England as it was when
Woolman saw it.

External ly it looks more like a dwelling-house than a meeting
place – probably due to a desire to be in harmony with other houses
next to it. An impressive wooden pillar in the middle of the room
was probably originally a ship's mast and the four-tiered platform
is unique: Hertford Meeting House has been remarkably well kept.

From Hertford, Woolman went to Baldock (19th June),
Sherrington (the 24th), Northampton (the 25th) and then to
Banbury where Oxfordshire's Quarterly Meeting was held 30th
June. There is a reference to Woolman at the Women's Quarterly
Meeting:

> We have had a very comfortable visit from our Friend John
> Woolman from America, whose tender advice and exhortation
> to Friends in general and the youth in particular will, we
> earnestly hope, remain sealed upon the minds of all present.[149]

From 1st July, Woolman was at Shipston, Warwick and
Coventry (exact dates not known) and then at Birmingham on the
17th. In a letter from William Forster to a cousin in Settle we read:

John Woolman left Birmingham the day I got in. He was at their meeting the day before where he appeared some time and to much satisfaction principally cautioning Friends against being too much engaged in worldly affairs ...[150]

Later Forster wrote a cousin in America:

The remarkable appearance of your countryman John Woolman who is now with Sarah Morris and her niece in Yorkshire, attracts the notice of many. His steady uniform deportment, his meekness and unaffected humility, his solidity, no less in conversation than in his ministry, which is instructing and edifying, creates much esteem and well corresponds with his appearance. I think your ministers in general far exceed ours though we are favoured with several eminent ones ...[151]

Another interesting letter concerns Woolman's visit to Sheffield. From Birmingham, Woolman went on to Nottingham (26th July), Oxton (the 28th), Mansfield (the 29th), Chesterfield (the 30th), Handsworth Woodhouse (the 31st) and Sheffield on the 2nd of August. The letter from Sheffield was written by Tabitha Hoyland and addressed to Sarah Tuke. Like some others Tabitha Hoyland referred to Woolman as 'Woolmer': a far more common name. She said:

... Our valuable Friends John Woolmer and Sarah Morris were at this meeting yesterday, was a week, which was exceedingly crowded, part through curiosity to see John's particular dress, and part I hope from a better motive, whom I apprehend went away well satisfied with what they heard from the man whose uncouth appearance will be likely to prejudice many. But he is certainly a very deep minister that searches things quite to the bottom, greatly exercised in a life of self-denial and humility. Therefore must the will of the creature be more subdued and the better fitted to receive the mystery of the kingdom, which I believe through much obedience are largely opened. And I can't but think Providence hath some wise end in what seems difficult to reconcile with man's wisdom. Perhaps it may be intended as a means to wean many from the things which outwardly adorn the body, and likewise other luxuries and delicacys, too much prevailing amongst those in exalted stations as to this world's enjoyments, besides the testimony he apprehends it a duty to bear against the iniquitous trading in Negroes that so deeply affected his mind as to make his tears both as meat and drink for many days ...[152]

Another letter about Woolman's Sheffield visit is dated 2nd August but the author is unknown; it appeared in Mary Andrews' *Book of Extracts* dated 1812. The author described Woolman's countenance as

> grave, sensible (sensitive) and expressive; in conversation rather reserved (except with a few individuals) being at all times more ready to hear than to offer the sacrifice of fools. Though many might think him whimsical from the odd appearance he made – he was a man of great understanding, and had very good natural abilities; of a mild and benevolent disposition, as might be easily discovered by the natural unaffected simplicity of his manners, which never failed of procuring respect, from all who were acquainted with him.[153]

Earlier the author gave a description of Woolman's clothing we have earlier alluded to, but added:

> He said the cause why he appeared so, was that he believed it to be his duty, to bear a testimony not in words only, but to be a sign to the people, to testify against the pride and extravagancy of those days, which greatly abounded with superfluities.
>
> He avoided the company of the rich and great, and would visit the habitations of the poor (who were well esteemed) with pleasure; he loved to see the honest simplicity of those who lived in remote parts of the world, and who were not over-anxious after riches, etc. His diet was plain, chiefly consisting of bread, milk or butter and he was truly a valuable, good man, a friend and well wisher to mankind universally, of whom it might be said, 'an Israelite indeed, in whom was no guile' ...[154]

From Sheffield Woolman was on to High Flatts (4th August), Huddersfield (the 5th), and Rushworth (the 9th). He was now in Yorkshire, a very large county then, and with his arrival at Settle, in the heart of 1652 country. Coming from Rushworth Woolman would have been very near Pendle Hill, one of the great places of Quaker pilgrimage where in 1652 George Fox had his vision of 'a great people gathered'. It seems likely Woolman went there but as he gave no 'sight-seeing' in his *Journal* we do not know. Settle's

Meeting House (1678) is another of the few basically as Woolman would have known it.

At Settle (16th August) Woolman interrupted his bare listing of places visited with a commentary on the prices of various articles and the wretched wages of the poor. The anonymous writer at Sheffield was right about his desire to 'visit the habitations of the poor'. Among other things he said wheat cost about 8 shillings, mutton 3 to 5 pence per pound, bacon from 7 to 9 pence. House rent for a poor man was from 25 to 40 shillings per year. Wood for fire was 'very scarce and dear'; coal in some places 2 shillings, 6 pence per hundred weight – 'but near the pits not a quarter so much'; all of which he commented: 'Oh, may the wealthy consider the poor!'

The reason was obvious because he then went on to relate that the wages of labourers in several counties toward London was 10 pence per day 'in common business' and

Industrious women who spin in the factories get some 4 pence, some 5 pence and so on ... Great numbers of poor people live chiefly on bread and water in the southern parts of England and some in the northern parts, and many poor children learn not to read. May those who have plenty lay these things to heart!

Then Woolman returned to an earlier concern. As his journey 'hath been without a horse' he received several offers from stagecoaches – but he would not accept them. Again he spoke of his scruple: 'it is common for horses to be killed with hard driving, and many others driven till they grow blind.' The postboys also faired poorly: 'Some boys who ride long stages suffer greatly in winter nights, and at several places I have heard of their being froze to death.'

Woolman was also again troubled by the slave trade and Quaker involvement:

I have felt great distress of mind since I came on this island, on account of the members of our Society being mixed with the world in various sorts of business and traffic carried on in impure channels. Great is the trade to Africa for slaves! And in loading these ships abundance of people are employed in the factories, amongst whom are many of our Society!

Next Woolman went to Lancaster; he did not mention it in the *Journal* but we know he was there before going north to Preston Patrick where he stayed three days (23rd-28th August). From Lancaster Sarah Hall wrote that Woolman was at

> this weekday meeting. He left the town that afternoon. After dinner Cousin Molly Bradford and I went to Cousin Dilworth's to see him. We had not sat long before he appeared beautifully indeed and very encouragingly. Glad we were that we went.

> He chose to walk. He was very particular in his dress. He wore a coarse cloth like flannel, no cuffs to his coat, a drab hat, a coarse unbleached shirt, no stock or neck-cloth, white woolen stockings, shoes uncurried, the native color, tied with the same. He drank no foreign liquors or tea. He did not choose to drink out of silver or make use of silver spoons. Herb tea sometimes he drank, sweetened with honey. Sugar he never chose. He was indeed a striking pattern of temperance and humility.[155]

Woolman said that at Preston Patrick he 'dreamed of mother.' Three days later he recorded in his *Journal* the vision he had when ill with pleurisy earlier discussed. We have little information of Woolman's time in Westmorland County other than that he rested a few days at Preston Richard at the home of George and Jane Crosfield. As earlier mentioned, Woolman had met Jane Crosfield during her travels in America.

Woolman was at Kendal on the 28th of August and at Greyrigg on the 30th; then he was over to Countersett in Yorkshire on the 6th of September. Again we have little information of these visits, but a letter in his hand to John Wilson at Kendal where he stayed was sent from York, 22 September. John Wilson is interesting in one particular respect: he was a 'shearman dyer' – dressing with shears and dying wool, one of the largest trades in Kendal. Woolman wrote his former host what Cadbury calls 'a gentle and belated caution':

> When I was at your house, I believe I had a sense of the pride of people being gratified in some of the business thou followest, and I feel a concern in pure love to endeavour to inform thee of it.[156]

111

Again Woolman's soft approach: we cannot help but wonder how the all-white Woolman felt surrounded by so much Kendal dye. Perhaps as Cadbury suggests he was thinking of Kendal when he said in his *Journal*: 'In these journeys I have been where much cloth hath been dyed and sundry times (have) walked over ground where much of their dye stuffs have drained away.'[157]

Woolman attended meeting at Countersett which he described as 'a large meeting house and very full ...' Little has changed of the building constructed in 1710 except that it is now rare to have a 'full' meeting; today meeting for worship is only on the first Sunday in each month. Nearby at Carr End lived the senior John Fothergill.

Woolman's progress to York was fairly slow: on the 13th of September he was in Richmond where he heard that his cousin William Hunt had died of smallpox a few days earlier at Newcastle. Woolman's next entry in his *Journal* was from York, but we know that he was also at Leyburn (possibly the 13th), Carlton Miniatt (the 16th), Thirsk (the 17th), Thornton-on-the-Hill (the 19th), Huby (the 20th) and Towthorpe (the 21st).

At Thirsk Woolman stayed with Robert Proud, the historian who had been a pupil of Dr John Fothergill. At this time Proud was back in Yorkshire in business with his brother. It is said that Proud asked Woolman where he intended to go after York. To which Woolman responded: 'I don't know. York looks like home to me.'[158] John Woolman would die there in three weeks' time.

Writers on Woolman have often spoken of his 'call to the North,' and in particular to Yorkshire. His certificate from Burlington Monthly Meeting mentioned Yorkshire by name and he had written 13th June from London to his wife: 'I have thought of going in a few days out of the city towards Yorkshire ...' Cadbury comments: 'The prior references to Woolman's concern point clearly to his interest in the northern areas [the "1652 county"], especially Yorkshire.'[159] Then Cadbury adds: 'Why the concern focused on this area we do not know, and perhaps Woolman did not know.'[160]

Over the years there have been more than hints from observers that Woolman had a premonition that he would die in York and much has been made of the fact that it was not far from York in

Richmond where he heard of the death by smallpox of his cousin William Hunt. But as previously noted, it is not in keeping with Woolman's character to make him into some sort of soothsayer; never once did he speak of his dreams in that fashion. Cadbury is right: we do not know and probably Woolman himself did not know why York looked like home.

It would be young Henry Tuke (aged 17), eldest son of William Tuke, who was sent to meet John Woolman as he approached the great walled

Henry Tuke (aged 17), as printed on page 19 of The Tukes of York *by E. M. and W. K. Sessions.*

city of York. Henry (1755-1814) known for his 'gentle and attractive ways' would forever be touched by his association with Woolman.

The Tukes of York were a remarkable family of Quaker innovators. Rowntree's great chocolate company originated in the family which also founded the Quaker Ackworth and Trinity Lane schools and the extraordinary mental hospital in York, The Retreat. As Maria Tuke Sainsbury writes:

> The first (Tuke) to emerge from the mists of antiquity being William Tuke ... His distinction in having turned men's thoughts towards a different manner of treating those of unsound mind. For disorders of the body the prevailing treatment was harsh, but for disorders of the mind it was cruel. A change was brought about by this Quaker, who was not a doctor ...

> William Tuke founded the Friends' Retreat at York in 1792, where the new ideas could be tried, and there they were proved so sound that gradually the great change was accomplished everywhere.[161]

In 1725, Mary Tuke started a shop which at first was at Walmgate, then Castlegate. In 1746, Mary was joined by the then

14-year-old William Tuke (her nephew); in 1754 he inherited the business. He turned the grocery shop into an important trade in tea, and at the same time William was a leading Quaker in the North. His first wife, Elizabeth Hoyland, died in 1760 after the birth of her fifth child. Henry was the oldest of the children – but only five when his mother died. William married his second wife, Esther Maud, in 1765; Rebecca Jones called her 'a Princess' and others said 'she remains as one of the Queens of Quakerism.' Her memorial was the York Girls School but she is also forever remembered for something else: nursing John Woolman during his fatal illness. We will shortly hear her words from his deathbed; like Henry she was greatly affected by Woolman.

Henry's son, Samuel, spoke movingly of his father's encounter with Woolman:

> That truly lowly and self-denying disciple of Jesus, John Woolman, came to York ... He travelled entirely on foot, and my father ... was sent to be his guide and companion ... I have frequently heard him speak of the indescribable sweetness of this walk, and of the satisfaction which he felt in the remembrance of it.[162]

Woolman had come to stay with the Tukes and to attend Quarterly Meeting at York, one of the larger ones in the country. It ran for three days – 22nd to 24th September, and originally Woolman intended to attend all the sessions. A letter from him on the 23rd gave no hint of what lay ahead: 'I am now at York at a Quarterly Meeting ... so well in health as to continue travelling ...'[163]

However, Woolman would not stay long with the Tukes at Castlegate which was right in the middle of the hustle and bustle of the city. Near the very end of his *Journal* writings he noted on the 28th September: 'Being now at the house of my friend Thomas Priestman ... so weak in body that I know not how my sickness may end ...' The entry was probably dictated by Woolman to Thomas Priestman.

The noise and smells of the busy narrow streets coming into the Tukes' otherwise pleasant abode affected him greatly. Unknown to himself and the Tukes he was in the first stages of the dreaded smallpox for which the incubation period is believed to be 10-14 days. Woolman asked if it were possible to find a quieter place and Esther Tuke immediately knew where he should go. Outside the city walls in Marygate were good friends Thomas and Sarah Priestman. Today the area has only a hint of being on the edge of the country; in Woolman's time it was a quiet retreat from city life. Almery Garth, the Priestmans' home, still stands and the section of the house – Littlegarth – where Woolman stayed has a memorial plaque to him.

Thomas Priestman's father was a tanner at Thornton-le-Dale and when his son came to York in 1762 he took to the same business. Almery Garth was an extensive property and a symbol of Priestman's success as a tanner. He had purchased it only five years before Woolman's visit. Thomas Priestman was a curious soul with decided tastes: he disliked umbrellas and tea and insisted that his sons drink home-brewed ale. But he was sincere, and despite his great house, rather plain. He detested ostentation and pride in

Woolman plaque in Littlegarth, off Marygate, York.

115

society and was an elder at York Meeting. Though he insisted his wife remain at home with the children, Sarah was also active in the Society of Friends.

When I was in York in 1997 I was privileged to visit the room at Littlegarth where Woolman died. He had selected it himself, and an 1842 description suggests that the room has not changed that much:

> Woolman fixed on this as being very quiet and retired, there being no thoroughfare at the back of the house except a footpath. It is just such a room as one might expect him to have chosen – whitewashed and without cornice or ornamentation of any kind ... It measured twelve by seventeen feet and its ceiling is nine feet high.[164]

Today it still is a bedroom – the bedroom of a young boy aged about five. When I was there you could easily recognize the recorded dimensions. But there is one addition which causes considerable surprise: in front of the bed is a pool table! And outside – the old footpath leads to the Marygate car park.

Auspiciously Woolman's *Journal* (the Moulton edition) ends with a dream about slavery. It was also probably dictated to Thomas Priestman and Woolman said the dream (or night vision) had been told to him by 'An honest-hearted Friend in America, who departed this life a little less than a year ago' and some months before the Friend died Woolman had heard it. Cadbury identifies the American Friend as Woolman's cousin Peter Harvey whom Woolman visited twice during his last illness. Woolman also spoke at Harvey's funeral.

In the dream Harvey had seen 'a great pond of blood from which a fog rose up. Some distance from him he saw this fog spread round about and great numbers of people walking back and forward in it.' Woolman perceived that Harvey understood that the pool of blood

> represented the state of those hardhearted men through whose means much blood is shed in Africa and many lives destroyed through insupportable stench and other hardships in crossing

116

the sea, and through extreme oppression bring many slaves to an untimely end.

The fog represented 'the gain arising on merchandise or traffic which many were taking hold of and, at the same time knew that the gain was the gain of oppression.'

Woolman said that Harvey 'had an inclination to see me' and asked to be with him in private and told his cousin he wished to express his feelings about the oppression of the slaves. Harvey did not feel 'easy to leave the world without opening to me.' How appropriate the dream would be at the end of the *Journal* and how typical of Woolman to tell us that, as he believed Harvey 'left no memorandum in writing of that dream or vision of the night, at this time I believe it seasonable for me to do it.' With those words the *Journal* ends.

Woolman's last public testimony was in a meeting for discipline at York Quarterly Meeting and it was on the subject of the slave trade. In a letter signed by William Tuke (but based on a record in which Thomas Priestman had collaborated) it was stated that Woolman remarked that

> as Friends had been solicitous for, and had obtained relief from many of their sufferings, so he recommended this oppressed part of the creation to their notice, that they may, in an individual capacity, as way may open, remonstrate their hardships and sufferings to those in authority, especially the legislative power in this kingdom.[165]

The record also shows that Woolman

> was enabled to attend all the sittings of (Quarterly Meeting) except the last ... The spring of the Gospel Ministry often flowed through him with great purity and sweetness as a refreshing stream to the weary travellers toward the city of God.[166]

Therefore Woolman returned to Almery Garth after the next to the last session. He never left Almery Garth again; as Cadbury says, 'scarcely the room or the bed.'[167] The Tukes and Priestmans took care of him and we know of his last days through William Tuke's record and Thomas Priestman's diary as well as a letter which Esther Tuke later wrote to Samuel Emlen.

As she said to Emlen 'no one was more with him, nor had greater opportunity to observe the state of his mind.' Esther Tuke's account of the illness was lengthy but moving. From her letter we read in part:

He was exceedingly afraid from the first of giving needless trouble to any; but his disorder increasing so much that constant attendance was necessary, he desired I would not sleep out of the house until I saw an alteration, which I very willingly complied with; and though it was exceedingly trying to see him labour under unspeakable affliction, and could render so little relief, yet I have many times been thankful in being favoured to attend him; for as I never saw one bear so much before, so I never beheld the like fortitude, patience and resignation – his hope and confidence were so strong and firmly fixed, that the greatest storms of affliction were not able to move him, or even cause him to utter an impatient word, indicating that he thought anything too hard; and though he was not free to take much medicines, yet he attended so much to the progress of the disorder, and his own feelings as to what was suited for healing or cooling nourishment ... that our apothecary (a man we think of singular judgment in that complaint, not a Friend) said he did not know he could be better ordered than he ordered himself; except towards the last, he seemed to feel the need of something more cordial, which he was not unwilling to take; but his throat was then so closed that he could not swallow, but with the greatest difficulty, and often strove, when it was distressing to see him, under his great weakness, and the pain it occasioned; and at times he quietly said, 'I believe I must in a little time give it over and try no more,' and it seemed twice wholly closed up.[168]

In another letter to a Friend whose name does not appear, Esther Tuke said:

The day before he died, his throat was closed up, that he could scarce speak intelligibly, which distressed me much, but in great measure removed this difficulty by asking for pen and ink, which we got and held the paper, and he wrote the words very legibly, though he was quite blind, and had been so for some days; twice his throat was quite closed, that he could not swallow one

118

drop of anything, and we had the most distressing prospect that he might continue some days in that situation. The Doctor syring'd his throat, but at last gave it up the night before he died, and said nothing could be done; but my husband, who will never give up using means as long as there is the least relief, set on to foment, with his consent; and continued it for two hours. He had a great satisfaction to find it open again, and he swallowed better than he had done for some days before, and we were ready to flatter ourselves with hope; but it was of short duration. For though he got a little ease in that respect, yet he was for several hours exceeding bad, and could not lie in bed. Was got up in a chair, and towards morning had on some of his cloaths, and with leaning on two, walked over the room; but wearied out, was laid down again upon the bed, and after some time, fell asleep; waked about the sixth hour, and breathed a few times, and departed without struggle, sigh, or groan.[169]

From the Tukes' accounts we know that three visitors were at the sick room of John Woolman during his last days. There were two apothecaries (one of whom Esther Tuke referred to as a 'Doctor') and appropriately, John Bispham of Mount Holly. In his article 'Who Paid for Woolman's Coffin?' Cadbury says of Bispham: 'There was little he could do in the two days before (Woolman's death) but after it he could at least fulfill Woolman's wish that York Friends be at no expense for the funeral.' Also 'Bispham was for the dying Woolman the only living link with home.'[170] All the American Quakers who had been at London Yearly Meeting in June were elsewhere.

As Woolman would have wished, the funeral was quite simple, and occurred two days after his death. At 'the large meeting' two Americans as well as Bispham were present: John Pemberton and Thomas Ross. Ross (1709-1786) came to Bucks County, Pennsylvania from Ireland as a young man. He never married and was described as 'sweet-spirited'. He had travelled to England in 1784 with Rebecca Jones and a serious fall on the voyage injured him so that he never fully recovered. He died near York in 1786 and was buried – at his own request – next to John Woolman.

Woolman's grave can still be visited at Bishophill Quaker Burial Ground in York. In the same ground are Thomas and Sarah

Priestman, William and Esther Tuke as well as Henry (William's son) and Mary Maria Tuke. In the 17th and 18th centuries it was Quaker practice not to have individual stones. But in Victorian times a practice of simple headstones began: round-topped with no decoration. They were all the same. Cadbury says that the present stone for Woolman 'goes back at least to 1888',[171] but there is an indication of an earlier one.

I visited the site in 1997 and using a picture from *The Wesleyan Methodist Magazine* (1910) I could see that Woolman's tombstone remained as stated 'at the foot of a tree'.[172] Appropriately someone had placed a bird box in the tree which had grown greatly since 1910. It was a cold and grey November day and I had made the mistake of wearing new shoes for the trip to York. My feet were full of blisters (perhaps akin to those of Woolman walking across England in 1772) and I felt foolish hobbling up Cromwell Road to Tuke House behind which the old burial ground – now a pleasant grassed area – serves as a garden for the Quaker housing trust. I had brought a little bouquet of red roses which I put down amongst the leaves in front of the headstone which says:

Near This Stone Rest the Remains of John Woolman of Mount Holly New Jersey North America Who Died at York 7th of 10th Month 1772 Aged 51 Years.

Perhaps it was a silly gesture but I remembered the words of John Greenleaf Whittier in 1871:

I have been awed and solemnized by the presence of a serene and beautiful spirit redeemed of the Lord from all selfishness, and I have been made thankful for the ability to recognise and the disposition to love him.[173]

And so did I.

*Bishophill Burial Ground, York. John Woolman's tombstone on right,
at foot of tree near wall.*
Courtesy of Wesleyan Methodist Magazine, London, 1910.

NEAR THIS STONE
REST THE REMAINS OF
JOHN WOOLMAN
OF MOUNT HOLLY
NEW JERSEY NORTH AMERICA
WHO DIED AT YORK
7th of 10th MONTH 1772
AGED 51 YEARS

John Woolman's gravestone.

121

Epilogue

Robert Frost once wrote:
Two roads diverged in a wood, and I –
I took the one less traveled by,
And that has made all the difference.[174]

IT WOULD BE HARD to imagine a figure more divergent from
John Woolman than my ancestor Daniel Boone, the most
famous American pioneer and a prototype of James Fenimore
Cooper's Leather-stocking. I should hasten to add, however, that
the popular image of Daniel Boone, the ripsnortin', tall-tale-tellin'
Indian fighter of American mythology has undergone a considerable metamorphosis.

Like his contemporary Woolman, Boone was raised in an 18th-
century Quaker environment; like the Woolmans, the Boones
emigrated from England for Penn's Holy Experiment. Daniel's
father, Squire Boone, arrived in Philadelphia with Quaker creden-
tials along with his brother George and sister Sarah. As the older
youth, they had been sent out earlier by their father to see what life
was like in the New World. On their advice, the larger Boone family
(including the younger children) arrived in 1717.

The Boones became charter members of the Preparative
Meeting at Exeter Township (named for their English market town
in Devon). Squire was the last member of the Boone family to go
to the Oley Valley; he was a bit of a fool, it seems, thinking that an
Indian attack on the settlement was imminent. After purchasing
250 acres at Oley and living there for twenty years, Squire was on
the move again; this time south to the Yadkin River Valley in North
Carolina. (Interestingly, Squire left the area at the same time John

Lincoln, another Quaker and the President's great-grandfather, moved west.)

While Squire's primary reason for moving was probably economic, he also had his problems with Quaker discipline and was 'read out of Meeting' by the Exeter meeting in 1748 for his unrepentance in allowing his son Israel to marry a non-Quaker. Generally the Boones were never notable members of the Society. Among others, Daniel's first cousin, Rosanna Boone, married German Lutheran immigrant, Martin Coulter. Coulter was my maternal great-great-great-great-great grandfather who arrived in Philadelphia in 1749 after his family lived for some years in Scotland.

As a boy I heard much about the Boones and our famous forbear (through two connections), Colonel Daniel Boone. My grandmother spoke reverently of a 'Boone Book' which carefully presented genealogy back to Daniel's time as if from Scripture itself. However, I never once heard of the Pioneer's Quaker background until much later in life, and then found it difficult to reconcile the American Indian fighter/folk hero image with Quakerism.

As with Woolman, Daniel Boone grew up in close proximity with Indians and took a keen interest in them. But their lives took radically different courses. Absent from the mythology surrounding Boone was the simple truth that to more gentrified settlers he and his companions were so influenced by the native American culture that they were viewed as 'white savages' or 'half-Indians'. As David Maurer has said:

> We often think of European culture as having overwhelmed the Native Americans, but in the realm of frontier hunter, it was quite the opposite. Europeans who lived in this milieu adopted a variety of native customs that formed the basis of a distinct subculture.[175]

Daniel Boone even looked like an Indian: deerskin smock cinched with a leather belt from which hung his bullet pouch, powder horn, knife and tomahawk. An Indian-style loincloth served as his shorts while deerskin leggings were held up by garters. His feet were shod in moccasins and like Indian men, his hair was long and plaited, shining with bear grease. Contrary to television

123

imagery, he did not wear a coonskin cap but a rather un-Indian looking headgear – a tall Quaker-style beaver hat, not unlike the man on Quaker Oats containers.

Like his compatriots Daniel Boone learned to hunt from the Indians. Often forgotten is that most settlers had no knowledge whatsoever of hunting: in Europe that was still the preserve of nobles and aristocrats. Trapping, tracking, calling, decoys and disguises were skills the Indians taught them.

Like his father, Daniel was restless and left North Carolina for Kentucky, then for settlers an unexplored wilderness. From 1769 he and his brother lived in forests like Indians and studied the lands. Twice he was captured by Indians; once adopted by the ferocious Shawnees, but he escaped both times. Boone had reason to hate the Indians as he lost two sons and a brother in Indian raids on the stockade he built at Boonesboro, the family settlement.

It was this point (settlement) which determined Boone's future course in dealing with the native population. The developing American obsession with private property came into direct conflict with the Indian culture of communal ownership and tribal economy. This was America's first ideological struggle, one destined to be won by the new settlers.

But as American Indian historian Paul Wallace writes:

Daniel Boone never became war-like, never surrendered himself to the hates and revenges that distorted the minds of many typical 'Indian killers'. He was first and last, a friend of the red race which he first met on the Shawnee Path in Oley. More than that, he never lost the respect and affection of these same people, who saw in him the qualities they most admired – warmth of heart, courage, devotion to duty and a straight tongue.[176]

At least in that sense some of his Quaker upbringing stayed with Daniel Boone.

However, as Wallace and others stress, in laying out the Wilderness Road, crossing the mountains into Kentucky, he 'more than any other' opened that 'Dark and Bloody Ground' – as the Indians came to call it – to settlement, and, of course, to the destruction of their native culture.

Unlike Woolman, Boone lived to an old age; his later years were spent near St Louis, Missouri where the only portrait of him from life was made. In it Boone appeared a somewhat philosophical and venerable frontiersman; much of the rough edge worn away with little trace of the earlier 'white savagery'. He was 86 when he died, and had outlived Woolman by 35 years. Ironically, Boone too had been exposed to the smallpox which took Woolman, but Boone's imperil was intentional. During an epidemic in Oley when Daniel was a boy he and his siblings were confined at home. Daniel did not like the restraint so one night he and a sister sneaked out of the house and spent the night in the bed of a stricken child. Soon thereafter both children came down with the disease but both were nursed back to health.

Not long after Boone's death in 1820, and during President Andrew Jackson's wholesale Indian displacement, Boone's image was transformed into a macho, Indian-hating frontiersman. This was largely due to the most popular biography of ante-bellum America: Timothy Flint's highly inventive life, which – even my relatives – took as gospel truth. Precious little of the original Quaker survived the transformation, and Flint's work was a good example of the words from the John Ford movie, *The Man Who Shot Liberty Valence*: 'When the legend becomes fact, print the legend.'

The metamorphosis continued as Daniel Boone was the thinly disguised model for the character Natty Bumppo in James Fenimore Cooper's *The Last of the Mohicans*. Interestingly, Cooper (1789-1851) was born into a Quaker family near Woolman's home territory at Burlington, but Cooper grew up in latter-day Boone fashion on the family frontier settlement called Cooperstown in New York State. The Coopers were among the English Quakers who settled in West Jersey around 1680. James Fenimore Cooper began writing only after being expelled from Yale and serving in the Navy for a brief period.

I have called John Woolman the quintessential Quaker: indeed he was the 'sweetest flowering of the Quaker spirit.' That spirit never flowered with some Quaker sons and daughters in America, and increasingly, as we have seen, American Quakerism became a peripheral body often turning inward on itself. Perhaps, it is just as well its numbers remained small: so often in American soil religious traditions – as with individuals – underwent metamorphosis.

In an environment which gloried in 'the right to bear arms', pushed native cultures to the brink of extinction and perfected capitalism into an American creed, the likes of John Woolman remain – as my father used to say – 'out in left field somewhere.' A number of well known Americans were raised in Quakerism, and either discarded the tradition on the road to success or discovered that several Quaker precepts were considerable handicaps. Aside from Boone and Cooper there were Thomas Paine, Dolley Madison and Benjamin West; and later (to some it comes as a shock), the only two Presidents with direct Quaker ancestry were Herbert Hoover and Richard Nixon.

Today James Fenimore Cooper's home at Burlington is a shrine, and Daniel Boone's Memorial, the Homestead, attracts many tourists and proclaims Boone as 'the greatest of American pioneers.' On 1 November 1938, the Boone Homestead was dedicated to 'the American Boy' and appropriately Boy Scouts assembled in great numbers; the American flag was raised by the Patriotic Order of the Sons of America and a great pageant based on Timothy Flint's mythology was presented.

John Woolman's modest Memorial in Mount Holly was established in 1915 when a small house on Branch Street was purchased in the belief that it was the house Woolman had built for his daughter Mary after she married John Comfort. However, later research revealed that it was the house of Jabez Woolston and his wife Esther who purchased the lot from John and Mary Comfort. But the land was Woolman's and today the Memorial property leads into his old apple orchard (now partially restored) and over to a white-pillared house on a hill, foundations of which shelter the remains of Woolman's home in Mount Holly.

Aside from the Woolman Memorial in his hometown, there also is Woolman Street, Woolman Commons – and even Woolman Lake. Finding the ancestral Woolman home near the Rancocas where he was born is a trickier matter. Driving on a narrow lane near Interstate 295 can be found the Granville Haines House named after a direct descendant of Woolman's grandfather. Apparently the present house incorporates the foundation walls

126

and bricks of the earlier 1703 structure. The Granville Haines House has sweeping views of the Rancocas, but another busy road, Highway 295, also cuts through the property. Passing through a tunnel under the highway, however, you come to a view of the great stream much in the manner which Woolman would have known it.

In the old cemetery of Mount Holly Meeting House (1775) is the burial place of Woolman's wife, and next to it a marker to him saying: 'Buried in York, England; Quaker Saint.' The old school house built in 1759 (where once Woolman probably taught) has been beautifully restored by the Colonial Dames of America. Not far from the school is the Three Tuns Tavern (1723) still used as a pub by the locals. Up from it, is the site of John Woolman's shop where a plaque tells us that there 'he probably tended shop and kept books in 1740 when a lad of 20.' We are also told that Woolman 'deeded it to his mother Elizabeth Woolman in 1753.' The older meeting house (1763) – the one Woolman would have known – was at the rear of the property and was in use until 1776, but nothing remains.

When I visited Mount Holly in March 1998, and stayed at the Memorial (there are three fine bedrooms upstairs) I was curious about the memory of Woolman in his hometown. I asked several residents if they thought the average Mount Holly citizen was aware of his significance. Some appeared surprised by the question as his name appears so often in town. One or two knew what I was getting at and admitted that, aside from the Quakers, they thought most people 'hadn't a clue.'

But Americans love their heritage in their own way – especially the colonial days, and there is almost a humourous compulsion to gentrify the colonial founders. This is clearly in full force at Peachfield Plantation, the ancestral home of Woolman's grandfather, Henry Burr, now a property of the Colonial Dames and their New Jersey headquarters. Recently an enormous Woolman geneaology was published and is on sale at the Memorial. At first it seemed to me wonderful that people would glory in discovering they might be related to John Woolman. But then you realize how generally Americans are obsessed with family trees: my cousins revel in the Daniel Boone connections. And it doesn't really matter just who the person is – as long as he is famous. I could not help but wonder what some of Woolman's descendants made of his radicalism.

I soon discovered that I had not far to go to find an answer in Mount Holly. Today the town is divided over a recent sociological development. The Mount Holly Presbyterian Church is very socially conscious and involved with the homeless and drug addicts of Burlington County – the largest of counties in New Jersey covering a diverse economic population. One centre in Mount Holly, 'The Mustard Seed', is a residence for 'families in transition', and one Presbyterian elder in particular has been active in providing local accommodation for 'society's rejects.' What would John Woolman's reaction be to the criticisms raised in his hometown that a quiet town has become a haven for 'dropouts' with – as it is claimed – an attendant rise in the local crime rate? Arguments heard were that 'they don't want to work' or 'just want to live off others.' Where would John Woolman stand in Mount Holly in 1998? Obviously – right in the middle of those 'undesirables', and extremely uncomfortable to discover that the more privileged were more interested in knowing whether or not they were related by birth to Mount Holly's most famous son.

Ultimately, the exercise of 'what would John Woolman do if he were alive today' is a dicey one, and probably my American history professor was right when he said that 'all what if's remain what if's.' However, in 1987 Canadian Keith Helmuth wrote a highly imaginative and provocative pamphlet *If John Woolman Were Among Us: Reflections on the Ecology of Flush Toilets and Motor Vehicles.* Unlike former commentators Helmuth stressed Woolman's 'gift of relational perspective, an ecological consciousness.'[177]

Helmuth also visited Mount Holly and was 'pleased to see' it was 'still a quiet town of small houses and shops.' He said that he

> could visualize John Woolman's apple trees and his tailor shop ... But all the while I was aware of the ceaseless churning commotion of the high energy industrial-commercial corridor throbbing around me. It was obvious, as I shut the gate to the grounds surrounding the small house that, exactly as Woolman saw it in his time, so it still is in ours; the desire for 'outward greatness' leads to social and ecosystem degradation.[178]

128

Helmuth chose to highlight two technologies – flush toilets and motor vehicles – because 'they rarely come up for serious consideration.' He feels that both 'force us to the level of ... ecological thinking that John Woolman used to such good effect.'[179] Helmuth thinks that if John Woolman were among us he would focus on 'the spiritual roots of our environmental crisis as he was on the spiritual roots of slavery and the socio-economic maladaptation of his time.' And Helmuth has an excellent analogy between the black slavery of Woolman's day and our 'vast array of fossil-fuel-powered energy slaves which have allowed us to avoid ecologically sound adaptation, and are, in fact, kicking the pins right out from under the biosphere.'[180]

Others too have noted Woolman's relevance to environmental issues as well as the counter culture we knew so well in the 1960s and 1970s which has re-appeared today only marginally. Phillips Moulton says that although Woolman's teachings are directed primarily to individuals, they also 'imply social criticism – particularly of an economic system which intensifies the profit motive.'[181] He cites an uncomfortable example of how people are encouraged to exploit both nature and their fellows for personal gain: 'note,' he says 'how certain arms manufacturers oppose the control of hand guns and how they rejoice when sales increase – instead of recoiling in horror at the murders and assassinations this facilitates.'[182] And that was written in 1973!

Gun control, modern man's madness over motor vehicles, the environment, the call to the simple life in face of greed and excessive profits: to what other concerns can Woolman be attached? His name is rightly honoured by British and American environmental groups – especially the Quaker Green Concern and the Friends Committee on Unity with Nature of North America. Anne Adams, the indomitable secretary of QGC, speaks of Woolman as 'the first ethical consumer'.

But also, as so frequently seen in the pages of the *Journal*, John Woolman remains to all who love animals our patron saint. Concern for 'the brute creation' has had a longer history in Quakerism than some have supposed. George Fox said that we should 'leave the creatures as we found them' and 'use the creatures in their service';

he even recognized that man had 'corrupted' the creatures by his abuse.

Early Friends were known for their kindness to animals and Thomas Clarkson (who was not a Quaker but campaigned against slavery in the 19th-century) observed that animals belonging to Friends were 'treated with a tender consideration and not permitted to be abused.'

Certainly next to Francis of Assisi, Woolman is the most appealing religious spokesman for God's creation. It was Woolman who at a tender age was 'seized with horror' at having killed a mother robin; who later was unwilling that a calf or lamb should be bled to death; and in England walked on foot rather than use a service which sometimes ran horses to death; and even on board ship was moved by the suffering of fowls accompanying passengers. So well known was Woolman's love of animals that it was mentioned at the memorial for him at his Meeting in Burlington. John Comfort spoke of the day when he and his father-in-law were harvesting a field and Woolman discovered blood on his scythe realizing that he had killed or injured some creature hidden in the grain. 'Such was his distress,' said Comfort that he called off his labourers to assist him in making search for it. The circumstance affected him so deeply that he did not recover from the pain it occasioned for a considerable term afterwards.[183]

Writing about a saint is not easy: sometimes John Woolman appears too good to be true. For generations used to having heroes with varying feet of clay, Woolman remains 'a pure and high spirit'.[184] The first booklet I read about Woolman was written in 1926 by F. V. Morley, and it opens by saying: 'Some say that John Woolman was a man in a manner divine; and some, that he is reminiscent of Uncle Joseph, in Stevenson's story *The Wrong Box*.'[185] Today that allusion sends one to Robert Louis Stevenson's eccentric character Joseph Finsbury who was 'shod with the health boot; his suit was of genuine ventilating cloth; his shirt of hygenic flannel, a somewhat dingy fabric ...'[186] But aside from peculiar clothing readers would search in vain for similarities between the two. Uncle Joseph did take on orphans and travelled around, but his bizarre character was genuinely oddball – and not very redeeming.

Vida Scudder, however, in her Introduction to the Everyman's Library edition of Woolman's *Journal*, discussed Woolman's 'absurdity' in an entirely different manner:

> ... the process in which he was engaged reached out to limits beyond our power to scan, and his experience is in one point of view an heroic *reductio ad absurdum*. No more instructive attempt was ever made to attain personal purity while neither withdrawing from the world nor transforming it.[187]

Scudder appears to feel that those were the only two options open for Woolman – or us. She says that Woolman 'was in an impasse' and 'while we love and reverence' his sturdiness of soul we

> must recognise with amusement touched by tenderness the hopelessness of his efforts to attain personal purity, the ridiculous extreme of isolation into which such a conscientious effort, if logically carried out, would lead us.[188]

Scudder misses the point of Woolman's method and influence which we have previously noted; what Michael Heller termed Woolman's 'soft persuasion' which eventually – and effectively – led Quakers and others to speak out and act against slavery and other injustices.

Phillips Moulton could have been directly addressing Vida Scudder when he wrote: 'Large scale social action is readily appreciated, but the purity of one's own soul is likely to be considered too trivial to warrant serious attention. Woolman thought otherwise.'[189]

Ultimately all of this is at the heart of any evaluation of Woolman's witness. His is a paradox as old as the Christian gospel itself. In 1824, Henry Crabb Robinson, the barrister and diarist, took an interest in Woolman. Robinson knew or corresponded with many of the major literary figures of his day, including Coleridge, Wordsworth, Blake and Lamb. From Lamb's library he was introduced to Woolman's *Journal* which he described 'A perfect Gem!' Robinson also is the one who called Woolman 'a beautiful soul'. However, he also remarked that had Woolman 'not been so very humble, he would have written a still better book; for fearing to indulge in vanity he conceals the events in which he was a great actor.'[190]

Yes, but as we have seen it is possible to reconstruct some of those events. We do not have as much as we would desire – and never will – but, despite himself, John Woolman shines forth in his age as a remarkably prophetic soul. Daniel B. Shea speaks to this point and, in a sense, presents the best last word on Woolman and his *Journal* and the effects of his self-effacement:

> It would not have occurred to Woolman that in his prose, ... he revealed himself as fully as later autobiographers more enamored of their individuality. His efforts to withdraw from the reader's view result finally in a self-portrait whose art is its transparency; the central actor of his narrative is no less compelling a figure for his reluctance to take the stage. What Woolman excludes, after all, he had defined as nonessential, exaggerated, or self-exalting; and few autobiographers have written whose knowledge of their subject was more honest or complete.[191]

The morning I left Mount Holly I was awaken by an unreal noise coming from several over-sized cars approaching Branch Street. I sat up in bed – one that could have belonged to Abner Woolman for all I knew. I had used his desk downstairs the night before. I later learned that the noise came from 'Boom-boxes', the latest American car accessory which, as the name suggests, creates an outrageous volume of 'music'. Over coffee I read the newspaper with accounts of more environmental disasters and an especially chilling report of a school child shooting some playmates on a playground.

That was *not* the note upon which I wished to leave John Woolman's hometown. I went out for a little walk down through Johnny's apple orchard. The trees would soon flower, and a robin was building a nest in one of them. A robin: full circle. Sentimental fool that I was, I took that as a good omen.

'All who read Woolman have a chance to realize that the best thing in the world is a really good person.'[192]

132

John Woolman Memorial, Mount Holly.

The author at work at Mount Holly.

Notes and References

1 *Nexus* (the Alumni Magazine of Boston University School of Theology), Vol. XV, Winter 1972, p.36.
2 Quoted on book jacket of Oxford University Press's 1971 Phillips P. Moulton edition *The Journal and Major Essays of John Woolman*. Henry Crabb Robinson called Woolman *schöne seele* and Sterling Olmsted used 'mystic and activist' as the subtitle to his Pendle Hill Pamphlet No. 312.
3 Moulton, Phillips P., *The Living Witness of John Woolman*, Wallingford, Pa., 1973, p.3.
4 Cady, Edwin, *John Woolman* (Great American Thinkers Series), New York, 1965, p.164.
5 Canby, Henry Seidel, *Classic Americans*, New York, 1959, p.29. This is 'a study of eminent American writers from Irving to Whitman' and places Woolman into an interesting context.
6 Priestland, Gerald, *My Pilgrim Way* (edited by Roger Toulman), London, 1993, p.26.
7 Cooke, Alistair, *America*, London, 1973, p.87.
8 Loukes, Harold, *The Quaker Contribution*, London, 1965, p.67.
9 Perinchief, Elizabeth Marren, *Henry Burr and His Heirs*, Colonial Dames of America, New Jersey, 1988, p.8.
10 Cady, *John Woolman*, p.53.
11 Ibid, p.56.
12 Green, Thomas, *John Woolman: a Study for Young Men*, London, 1897, p.7.
13 Whitney, Janet, *John Woolman: Quaker*, London, 1943, p.34. Sadly Mrs Whitney's narrative form almost 'sinks' her work, but there are some excellent sources and comments throughout the book.

[14] Ibid.
[15] Levy, Barry, *Quakers and the American Family: British Settlement in the Delaware Valley*, New York, 1988, from the introduction on the book jacket. Highly recommended study.
[16] Tindall, George Brown and Shi, David Emory, *America: a Narrative History*, New York, 1984, p.78.
[17] Ibid, p.80.
[18] Snell, Beatrice Saxon, *John Woolman: Conscientious Affirmer*, London, 1967, p.7. This delightful pamphlet is well worth reprinting.
[19] Cooke, *America*, p.72.
[20] Cady, *John Woolman*, p.68.
[21] Moulton, Phillips P., (ed.), *The Journal and Major Essays of John Woolman*, Richmond, Indiana, 1989, p.314.
[22] Tindall and Shi, *America*, p.87.
[23] Marietta, Jack D., *The Reformation of American Quakerism 1748-1783*, Philadelphia, 1984, p.127.
[24] Ibid, p.128.
[25] Whitney, *John Woolman*, p.115.
[26] Drake, Thomas, *Quakers and Slavery in America*, New Haven, Conn., 1950, p.56.
[27] Brinton, Howard, in his chapter, 'Dreams of Journalists' in *Byways in Quaker History*, Wallingford, Pa., 1944, p.209.
[28] Olmsted, Sterling, *Motions of Love: Woolman as Mystic and Activist*, Wallingford, Pa., 1993, p.28.
[29] Gummere, Amelia Mott (ed.) *The Journal and Essays of John Woolman*, London, 1922, p.51.
[30] Marietta, *Reformation*, p.144.
[31] Snell, *John Woolman*, p.10.
[32] Tindall and Shi, *America*, p.121.
[33] Walvin, James, *The Quakers: Money and Morals*, London, 1997, p.104. Interesting study, very well written.
[34] Olmsted, *Motions of Love*, p.28.
[35] *Journal* of Joshua Evans (ed. by George Churchman), *Comly's Miscellany*, Vol. X, Philadelphia, 1837, p.34.
[36] Drake, *Quakers and Slavery*, p.60.
[37] Reynolds, Reginald, *The Wisdom of John Woolman*, London, 1977, p.163. No writer on Woolman has come closer to his spirit than Reynolds.

[38] Marietta, *Reformation*. See Marietta's introduction for his statement of intent.

[39] Tolles, Frederick B., *Meeting House and Counting House: The Quaker Merchants of Colonial Philadelphia, 1692-1763*, Chapel Hill, N.C., 1949.

[40] Whittier, John Greenleaf, Introduction to *Journal of John Woolman*, Glasgow, 1883, p.13.

[41] Ibid, p.15.

[42] Ibid.

[43] Peare, Catherine Owens, *John Woolman: Child of Light, the Story of John Woolman and the Friends*, New York, 1954, p.80. Another narrative biography.

[44] Ibid, p.15.

[45] *Journal* of John Hunt, *Friends Miscellany*, Vol. X, p.241.

[46] Reynolds, *Wisdom*, p.165

[47] Ibid.

[48] *Journal* of John Hunt, p.250.

[49] *Friends Miscellany*, Vol. IV (1787), p.276.

[50] Brookes, George S., *Friend Anthony Benezet*, Philadelphia, 1937, p.1.

[51] Ibid, p.39.

[52] Ibid, p.50.

[53] Ibid.

[54] Ibid.

[55] Whitney, *John Woolman*, p.40.

[56] Cadbury, Henry J., *John Woolman in England, 1772: a Documentary Supplement*, London, 1971, p.96. Authoritative and thorough.

[57] Brookes, *Friend*, p.45.

[58] Ibid, p.75.

[59] Ibid, p.84.

[60] Letter from Anthony Benezet to John Wesley, 23 May 1774.

[61] Brookes, *Friend*, p.138.

[62] Tolles, *Meeting House*, p.vii.

[63] Ibid.

[64] Ibid, p.109.

[65] Ibid, p.82.

66 Letter from Israel to John Pemberton, 7 June 1749 (Pemberton Papers V, 107).
67 Tolles, *Meeting House*, p.83.
68 Jones, Rufus M., *Quakers in the American Colonies*, London, 1911, pp.565-566.
69 Marietta, *Reformation*, p.32.
70 Whitney, *John Woolman*, p.264.
71 Gummere, *Journal*, p.542.
72 Reynolds, *Wisdom*, pp.167-168.
73 Moulton, *Living Witness*, p.7.
74 Whitney, *John Woolman*, pp.313-314.
75 Gummere, *Journal*, p.101.
76 *A First Book for Children*, Friends House Library, London.
77 Heller, Michael A., 'John Woolman's Soft Persuasion,' in *John Woolman's Spirituality and Our Contemporary Witness* (ed. by Shirley Dodson), Philadelphia, 1995, p.83.
78 Thomas, Hugh, *The Slave Trade: the History of the Atlantic Slave Trade, 1440-1870*, London, 1997, p.270.
79 Gummere, *Journal*, p.233.
80 Thomas, *Slave Trade*, p.270.
81 Drake, *Quakers and Slavery*, p.63.
82 Gummere, *Journal*, p.234.
83 Drake, *Slave Trade*, p.50.
84 *Friends Intelligencer*, 1902.
85 Marietta, *Reformation*, p.101.
86 Cooke, *America*, p.160.
87 Rivinus, Willis, *William Penn and the Lenape Indians*, New Hope, Pa., 1995, p.25. This is an especially valuable book as the author has such an excellent grasp of the Indians closest to early Quaker settlement. Highly recommended.
88 Ibid, p.2.
89 Ibid.
90 Jones, *Quakers*, p.496.
91 Rivinus, *William Penn*, p.59.
92 Josephy, Alvin M., *500 Nations: an Illustrated History of the North American Indians*, London, 1995, pp.235-236.
93 Corner, Betsey C. and Booth, Christopher C. (ed.), *Chain of Friendship: Selected Letters of Dr John Fothergill of London, 1735-1780*, Cambridge, Mass., 1971, p.24.

94 Shore, W.T., *John Woolman: His Life and Our Times*, London, 1913, pp.114-115.

95 Jones, *Quakers*, p.504.

96 Rivinus, *William Penn*, p.67.

97 Jones, *Quakers*, p.404.

98 Stuart Wavell in his review of *Wyatt Earp: The Life behind the Legend*, *The Sunday Times*, 4 January 1998 (Books Section), p.3.

99 As quoted in Josephy, *500 Nations*, p.250.

100 Whitney, *John Woolman*, p.304.

101 Ibid.

102 See Carroll, Kenneth L., 'The Influence of John Woolman on Joseph Nichols and the Nicholites' in *Then and Now: Quaker Essays: Historical and Contemporary* (ed. by Anna Brinton), Philadelphia, 1960, pp.168-179.

103 Middleton, Richard, *Colonial America: a History, 1585-1776*, (Second Edition), Oxford, 1996, p.201. Highly recommended.

104 Ibid, p.400.

105 See Numbers 13, 21; 14, 43ff; I Samuel 15, 27-30.

106 Middleton, *Colonial America*, p.163.

107 Walker, Williston, *A History of the Christian Church* (revised), New York, 1959, p.453.

108 Trueblood, D. Elton, *The People Called Quakers*, Richmond, Ind., 1971, p.159.

109 Lampden, John, 'John Woolman's Dreams' in *John Woolman's Spirituality...*, pp.25-26.

110 Whitney, *John Woolman*, p.343.

111 Moulton, *A Plea for the Poor* in his edition of the *Journal*, p.238.

112 Moulton, *Living Witness*, p.21.

113 Reynolds, *Wisdom*, p.136.

114 Ibid, p.141.

115 Moulton, *Plea*, p.238.

116 Reynolds, *Wisdom*, p.168.

117 Ibid, p.169.

118 Ibid, p.132.

119 Ibid, pp.134-135.

120 Whitney, *John Woolman*, p.345.

121 Ibid, p.347.

122 Barclay, John (ed.), *Lives of Samuel and Mary Neale, 1729-92,* London, 1845, p.167.
123 Gummere, *Journal,* p.565.
124 Barclay, John, *Joseph Oxley's Journal* in *A Select Series,* Vol. 5, London, 1837, p.384.
125 Cadbury, *John Woolman,* p.36.
126 Gummere, *Journal,* p.321f.
127 Cadbury, *John Woolman,* pp.30-31.
128 Ibid.
129 Whitney, *John Woolman,* p.357.
130 Gummere, *Journal,* pp.125-126.
131 Manuscript owned by Herbert Pickles, Jordans, Buckinghamshire.
132 Whitney, *John Woolman,* p.370.
133 Manuscript at John Woolman Memorial, Mount Holly, N.J.
134 Cadbury, *John Woolman,* p.46.
135 Ibid, pp.45-46.
136 Ibid, pp.46-47.
137 Corner and Booth, *Chain of Friendship,* p.385.
138 Cadbury, *John Woolman,* p.70.
139 Fox, R. Hingston, *Dr John Fothergill and His Friends,* London, 1919, p.385.
140 *The Friend,* Vol. 21, Philadelphia, 1847-48, p.337.
141 Cadbury, *John Woolman,* p.70 and Gummere, *Journal,* p.129.
142 Whitney, *John Woolman,* p.374.
143 Cadbury, *John Woolman,* p.43.
144 Ibid, p.50.
145 Ibid, p.52.
146 Ms. Vol. 163/4, Friends House Library, London.
147 Gummere, *Journal,* p.30.
148 Records of Hertford QM.
149 Records of Berkshire and Oxfordshire GM.
150 Ms. Vol. 77, p.1, Friends House Library, London.
151 Ibid, p.3.
152 Cadbury, *John Woolman,* pp.94-95.
153 Ibid, pp.95-96.
154 Ibid, p.96.
155 Ibid, p.102.
156 Ibid, p.110.

[157] Ibid, p.111.
[158] Whitney, *John Woolman*, p.395.
[159] Cadbury, *John Woolman*, p.82.
[160] Ibid.
[161] Sainsbury, Maria Tuke, *Henry Scott Tuke: a Memoir*, London, 1933, p.13. See also Sessions, E.M. and W.K., *The Tukes of York*, 1987.
[162] Cadbury, *John Woolman*, p.119 (from *Family Portraits: Memoirs of Samuel Tuke*, London, 1860).
[163] Gummere, *Journal*, p.141. (This letter is found in the back of *The Journal and Voyage to England* in John Woolman's hand, and is the copy made by himself.)
[164] Gummere, *Journal*, p.140.
[165] Cadbury, *John Woolman*, p.116.
[166] Ibid.
[167] Cadbury, *John Woolman*, p.117.
[168] Gummere, *Journal*, pp.145-146.
[169] Ibid, pp.148-149.
[170] Cadbury, Henry, 'Who Paid for Woolman's Coffin?', *Friends Journal*, Vol. 10, November 1964, p.495.
[171] Cadbury, *John Woolman*, p.128.
[172] See picture on page 511 of Gummere, *Journal*.
[173] Whittier, *Introduction*, p.49.
[174] Hamilton, Ian (ed.), *Robert Frost: Selected Poems*, London, 1973, p.77. (These lines are the final three of Frost's poem, *The Road Not Taken*.)
[175] Maurer, David, 'Daniel Boone's Pennsylvania Birthplace' in *Colonial Homes*, June 1994, pp.83 and 85.
[176] Wallace, Paul A., *Daniel Boone in Pennsylvania*, Harrisburg, Pa., 1987, p.10.
[177] Helmuth,Keith, *If John Woolman Were Among Us: Reflections on the Ecology of Flush Toilets and Motor Vehicles*, (Canadian Quaker Pamphlet No. 32), Argenta, B.C., 1994, p.1.
[178] Ibid, p.3.
[179] Ibid, p.39.
[180] Ibid, pp.8-9.
[181] Moulton, *The Living Witness*, p.12.
[182] Ibid.

183 Whitney, *John Woolman*, pp.319-320.

184 Scudder, Vida D. in her Introduction to *The Journal and Other Writings* (Everyman's Library), London, 1952, p.xvii.

185 Morley, F.V., *The Tailor of Mount Holly: John Woolman*, London, 1926, p.1.

186 Stevenson, Robert Louis, and Osbourne, Lloyd, *The Wrong Box*, New York, 1891, p.14.

187 Scudder, *Journal*, p.xvii.

188 Ibid, p.xviii.

189 Moulton, *Living Witness*, p.20.

190 Robinson, Henry Crabb, *Diary, Reminiscences and Correspondence*, (Thomas Sadler, ed.), Vol. II, London, 1869, p.266.

191 Shea, Daniel B., *Spiritual Autobiography in Early America*, Princeton, 1968, p.84. Shea's chapter on Woolman's *Journal* well discusses its unique qualities, but as Moulton pointed out, Shea 'is led into errors by his reliance on the Gummere edition.'

192 Trueblood, *The People*, p.167.

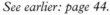

See earlier: page 44.

As printed on page 14 of More Quaker Laughter
by William H. Sessions.

Index

Sauer, Christopher, 60
Scarborough, John, 60
Scots-Irish (Scotch-Irish), 13, 30, 78, 84, 85
Scripture, interpretation of, 37-38
Scudder, Vida, 131
Separatists, 5
Setauket, 22
Settle (England), 107, 109-110
Shackamaxon 'treaty', 68
Shakers, 5, 81
Sharpe, Granville, 25
Shaw, George Bernard, 88
Sheffield (England), 108, 109
Shea, Daniel, 132
Sherrington (England), 107
Shipston (England), 107
Slavery, 14, 16-22, 23, 25, 37, 38, 39, 44, 45, 47, 50, 57, 60, 64, 67, 75, 84, 85, 94, 103, 110, 116-117
Sleeper, John, 60
Smallpox, 20, 62, 69, 115, 125; inoculation against, 62-63
Smith, John, 82, 83
Smith, William, 29, 30
Snell, Beatrice Saxon, 14, 30
South Carolina, 16, 19, 38
Sparks, Capt., 97, 104
Sperry, Willard, 1-2, 5
Stanley, James, 38; William, 38
Stanton, Daniel, 60
Stevenson, Robert Louis, 130
Swarthmore College (Pa.), 100
Sykes, John, 60

TEEDYUSCUNG, 72
Teresa of Avila, 1, 27, 85
Thirsk (England), 112
Thomas, Hugh, 64
Thornton-on-the-Hill (England), 112
Three Tuns Tavern (Mount Holly, N.J.), 127
Tobacco, 16, 38
Tolles, Frederick, 43, 52, 58
Townsend, John, 103, 104
Towthorpe (England), 112

Trueblood, D. Elton, 86
Tuke family, 113, 114, 117
  Elizabeth (née Hoyland), 114
  Esther (née Maud), 114, 115, 117, 118, 119, 120; letter to Samuel Emlen, 117-118; another letter, 118-119
  Henry (son of William), 113, 114
  Mary, 113
  Mary Maria, 120
  Samuel (son of Henry), 114
  William, 113, 114, 117, 120
Tuke House (York), 120

UNITARIANS, 85
Universalists, 85

VIRGINIA, 19, 38, 39, 52
  Yearly Meeting, 39

WALKING Purchase, 70
Wallace, Paul, 124
Walmgate (York), 113
Walvin, James, 34
War tax, 29, 30
Warwick (England), 107
Wavell, Stuart, 76
Wesley, John, 7, 21, 25, 50
West, Benjamin, 68, 79, 126
West Indies, 44, 67
White, Joseph, 95
Whitefield, George, 21, 22, 39, 50, 62
Whitney, Janet, 9, 54, 59, 60, 79, 87, 92, 96, 102
Whittier, John Greenleaf, 44, 120
Wilderness Road, 124
Wilson, John, 111
Wilson, Rachel, 92, 93
Witchcraft, 27
Woolman, Abner (brother of JW), 9, 60, 65, 132
  Asher (brother of JW), 9, 60, 79
  Elizabeth (née Burr; mother of JW), 6, 7, 10, 20, 111, 127
  Elizabeth (sister of JW), 5, 6, 9, 20
  John (son of JW), 24, 93

Map of John Woolman's travels on foot in England: June to November 1772.
Based on Henry J. Cadbury's *Documentary Supplement.*